Rocky Mountain News
RIDE GUIDE

Rocky Mountain News
RIDE GUIDE

Favorite Colorado Bicycle Routes
From The Weekly Column

DAVID NELSON

Denver Publishing Company

Printed in the United States of America

First Edition
ISBN 0-914807-10-2
Library of Congress Catalog Card Number 90-080699

Library of Congress Cataloging-in-Publication Data
Nelson, David
    Rocky Mountain News RIDE GUIDE, Favorite Colorado Bicycle Routes From TheWeekly Column
1. Bicycle touring – Colorado – Guide-books.
2. Bicycle touring – Rocky Mountains – Guide-books.
2. Bicycle touring – West (U.S.) – Guide-books.
I. Title.

Cover design by Jerry Lundwall
Cover photograph: Trail through wildflowers near
    Crested Butte, Colorado.
Cover photograph by Paul Gallaher

ROCKY MOUNTAIN NEWS *RIDE GUIDE*

TABLE OF CONTENTS

The Routes

The Routes (continued)

ACKNOWLEDGMENTS

In the course of riding and researching bicycle routes, I acquired valuable information and assistance from cyclists, friends, local and state government, the Forest Service, and countless others – to all, thank you.

Special thanks to Chris and the *Rocky Mountain News* for their support in publishing this book, to Bill for the inspiration, to Annie for proofreading and encouragement, to Jerry for cover design, to Wayne for his incredible bikes, to BBC, Inc. for numerous copies and laserprints, and especially to Phil for insisting I take a byte of the apple.

INTRODUCTION

Colorado means the outdoors. It means vigorous people finding healthy ways to enjoy the outdoors. It means, among other things, riding bicycles.

As editor of the *Rocky Mountain News*, I occasionally look at statistics about what Colorado residents like to do. A little more than a year ago, I happened across an interesting fact: Denver residents purchase more bicycles per capita than residents of any other major city. The fact came as little surprise, of course. Walk around the city and open your eyes and there they are – bicycle riders by the dozens. Even on our coldest days, the kind that make your eyelashes brittle, there they are, pumping energetically along, enjoying mountain views and those Colorado skies of a special blue – and looking happier than ought to be legal.

Enter David Nelson. This very nice, very enthusiastic guy is the state's Mr. Bicycle. He is knowledgeable and involved, a bicycle promoter and a bicycle-event organizer. He is also the bicycle columnist for the *Rocky Mountain News*. When he knocked on our door and asked if we were interested in his columns, we said sure, you bet, but only if you can execute them well. He did. His detailed and accurate descriptions of Greater Denver bike trails, complete with maps, were an immediate hit with readers.

This book is a compilation of those columns, and if the plaudits of our readers mean anything, you will find them useful. That's true whether you are an accomplished hand at the sport or a beginner. So read the chapters, study the maps and get out there for a special kind of Rocky Mountain high, an aerobic high in the Colorado outdoors.

— Jay Ambrose, editor, *Rocky Mountain News*

PREFACE

All of the *RIDE GUIDE* bicycle routes featured in this book are as they appeared when printed in the weekly column in the *Rocky Mountain News,* except for minor changes to relevant information. The text and maps were believed to be accurate, and considerable research was conducted to confirm accuracy, at the time each column was first printed. Because of potential altering of stated signs or landmarks, especially on mountain roads and trails, I cannot absolutely assure all of the information is still accurate as stated. However, having ridden all of the routes numerous times, I am confident the information supplied is more than sufficient for enjoyable bicycle rides.

A brief discussion of the elements contained in each *RIDE GUIDE* column follows so as to convey a better understanding of my ratings, evaluations and recommendations:

BICYCLE: In every case where the route follows paved roads, a mountain bike can be substituted for a road bike. When a mountain bike is specified, however, a road bike should not be substituted.

SURFACE: Road and trail surfaces can change significantly depending on time of year and current weather conditions. Use this section to evaluate general riding conditions.

DISTANCE: Distances are deemed to be accurate to the nearest few tenths of a mile. They were measured with a properly calibrated bicycle computer and with an opisometer on a map.

DIFFICULTY: The rating as to difficulty is directed at the average ability, that is, neither a novice nor an expert cyclist, but somewhere in between. In most cases, I qualify my rating with information about steep grades, mileage and other factors to help you better apply the rating to your ability.

RIDE TIME: This section also addresses average ability. A moderate pace and rest stops are included in the suggested time allotment.

THE ROUTE: The directions and that which you may expect to encounter along the route are included; history, scenic vistas, flora and fauna, and geography are often part of this section. When warranted, certain elements are featured in their own, separate section.

MAPS: My route map should be used as a general locater map only. I recommend other, more detailed maps of an area. Always take a map with you when riding new routes.

SHIFTING GEARS: This is a catch-all section for tips, regulations, ethics, trivia and other information.

A final and short note on safety and comfort:

Make certain your bicycle is in proper operating condition and always carry tubes and/or a patch kit , a pump, tools, identification, money and water.

Don't second guess Colorado weather – be prepared for adverse conditions; <u>never</u> go on a ride without a windbreaker.

And no matter how much you hate to, please wear your helmet.

Adams County Loop

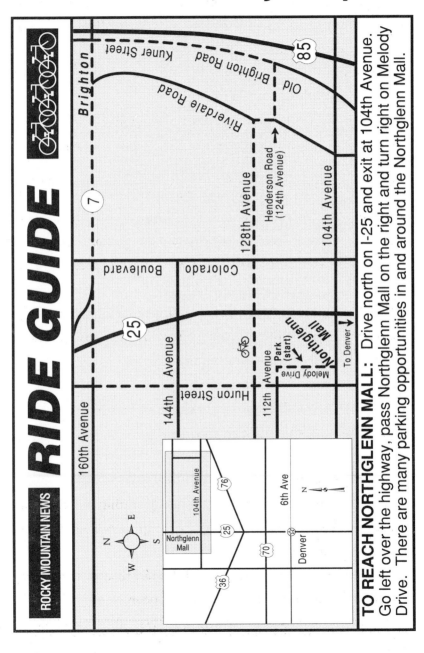

TO REACH NORTHGLENN MALL: Drive north on I-25 and exit at 104th Avenue. Go left over the highway, pass Northglenn Mall on the right and turn right on Melody Drive. There are many parking opportunities in and around the Northglenn Mall.

ROCKY MOUNTAIN NEWS *RIDE GUIDE*

BICYCLE: A road bike is preferable, but a mountain bike will do; the less knobby the tires, the better.

SURFACE: These Adams County roads are generally smooth. Huron Street has some rough spots, and the shoulders are narrow. Watch for sand in the spring.

DISTANCE: This loop is about 31 miles.

DIFFICULTY: The riding is easy to moderately difficult, mostly because of the mileage. There are two gradual climbs of several miles each.

RIDE TIME: Allow about two and a half hours to finish the ride.

THE ROUTE: This route will take you on a tour of the back roads of Adams County. The terrain and scenery vary dramatically from shopping mall to residential neighborhood to rural expanses with pockets of development. But look above all this for magnificent views of the Front Range.

My introduction to this loop from Northglenn Mall to Brighton and back came via John Holman and the Denver Bicycle Touring Club. Billed as a "frostbite ride", it's a route the club likes to ride in the winter, weather permitting. Our early March experience produced more bite from the sun than from frost.

From your parking place at the Northglenn Mall, find Melody Drive on the west side of the mall and head north. At approximately three quarters of a mile go left on 112th Avenue and immediately right on Huron Street.

Huron climbs gently for another six miles to 160th Avenue. Huron Street tapers to one lane in each direction and the shoulders are relatively narrow, so stay right and single file. The Sunday traffic was light.

To the west is the first scenic look at the Front Range. Keep your viewing to glimpses here and be alert for several slightly rough spots; there are better vistas ahead.

Go right on 160th Avenue and continue nearly nine miles into Brighton. Once you cross the Valley Highway and then merge into Route 7 (almost two miles from 160th), the road gradually climbs for about another seven miles. Take a right on Kuner Road; it's just before the Route 85 overpass, and well marked.

Kuner Road becomes Old Brighton Road as you head south. On this stretch of road there are some fast food restaurants if you're in need of fuel. Pedal five miles from 160th and go right (west) on Henderson Road (124th Avenue).

Henderson quickly runs into Riverdale. Go right and immediately bend to the left (west again) onto 128th Avenue. Follow 128th for another six miles back to Huron Street and go left and back to your car.

On 128th, the Front Range is right in your face and spectacular. Indian Peaks are slightly northwest, and further north a great view of Longs Peak. There is a park a half mile past Colorado Boulevard for a break.

Off 160th Avenue the ride can be shortened by going right on Riverdale Road. Riverdale is about a mile west of Brighton; follow it along the South Platte River for three and a half miles to 128th Avenue and go right.

Alderfer/Three Sisters

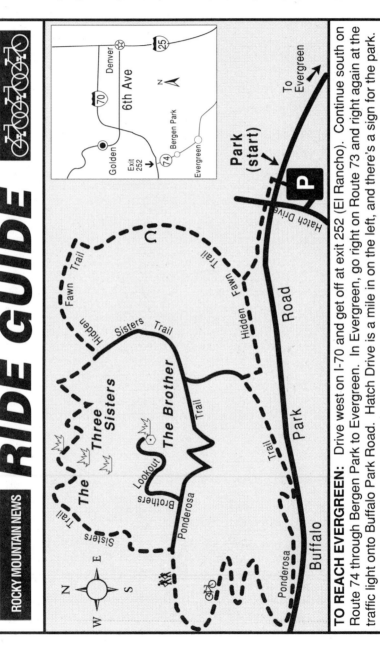

TO REACH EVERGREEN: Drive west on I-70 and get off at exit 252 (El Rancho). Continue south on Route 74 through Bergen Park to Evergreen. In Evergreen, go right on Route 73 and right again at the traffic light onto Buffalo Park Road. Hatch Drive is a mile in on the left, and there's a sign for the park.

ROCKY MOUNTAIN NEWS **RIDE GUIDE**

BICYCLE: This ride is for mountain bikes.

SURFACE: The single track hiking trails in the park are generally smooth. There are some mildly rocky sections, and several stretches of trail that include check bars, the logs across the trail that help prevent water erosion.

DISTANCE: A loop of the park is about three and a half miles. You can add more miles on the interior trails, or by taking another lap.

DIFFICULTY: The riding is easy to moderate; there are several short climbs with switchbacks. The route is not technically difficult, but requires some basic handling skills on the rocky and downhill sections.

WILDLIFE: The park supports a bird population that can include turkey vultures, hawks, flickers, jays, ravens, mountain bluebirds and other species.

THE ROUTE: The Alderfer/Three Sisters Park gets it name from the Alderfer family and the three rock outcroppings known as The Sisters. There is also one larger rock mass named The Brother.

The Alderfers have operated a cattle ranch in the area for some time and they donated land that makes up a portion of the park. The rest of the park, the northern part that includes the Three Sisters, was given by the Spencer Wyant family.

From the Wilmot School parking lot, cross Buffalo Park Road and go left (west) on the trail that follows the road. You'll gently climb for a quarter of a mile to the trailhead, where a map is available from the mapbox.

Continue up a tenth of a mile to the Hidden Fawn Trail and take a right (north). The path rolls along for a little more than half a mile as it bends back to the west and then intersects the Sisters Trail.

All the trails in the park cut through beautiful and rugged pine forest typical of the Pike and Arapaho National Forests. You'll get the feeling that you are deep in the backcountry, not just a few miles outside of Evergreen.

The first third of a mile on the Sisters Trail has several switchbacks; it's the steepest part of the ride. At the top, introduce yourself to the sisters and check out the scenery. To the northeast is a great view of Evergreen Lake.

Descend to the Ponderosa Trail and go right. On the Ponderosa you will start to the west, wind south and then eventually back to the east to join the Hidden Fawn again. Mount Spaulding, Mount Evans and Epaulet Mountain are visable to the west from the Ponderosa Trail.

Go right on the Hidden Fawn Trail for about two tenths of a mile and right again down the access trail to your car.

If you are feeling additionally inspired, go left, instead, at the bottom of the Ponderosa and left again back onto the Ponderosa for a climb up to Brothers Lookout. Take a right for the final ascent to another panoramic view of Evergreen and the surrounding area.

SHIFTING GEARS: In colder winter weather, make sure to keep your head and ears warm, but how do you fit a hat under your helmet? There are helmet liners made to do the job.

Argentine Pass

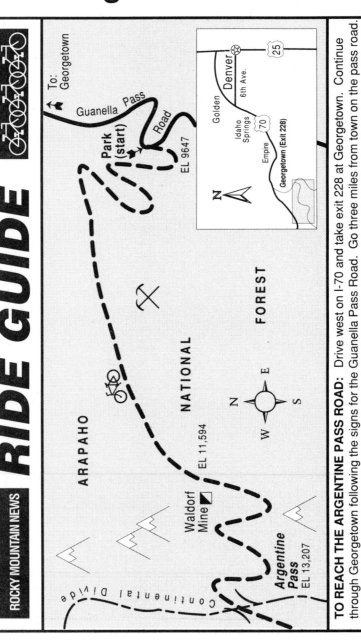

RIDE GUIDE

ROCKY MOUNTAIN NEWS

To: Georgetown

Guanella Pass

Park (start)

Road

EL 9647

Denver

Golden

6th Ave.

Idaho Springs

Empire

Georgetown (Exit 228)

Denver

25

70

N

ARAPAHO

NATIONAL FOREST

Waldorf Mine

EL 11,594

Argentine Pass

EL 13,207

Continental Divide

N

W — E

S

TO REACH THE ARGENTINE PASS ROAD: Drive west on I-70 and take exit 228 at Georgetown. Continue through Georgetown following the signs for the Guanella Pass Road. Go three miles from town on the pass road. Look for a cutout on a switchback with a dirt road heading north. (There's a chainlink fence.) Park on the cutout.

ROCKY MOUNTAIN NEWS *RIDE GUIDE*

BICYCLE: Mountain bike.

SURFACE: Smooth Forest Route and rocky, steep four-wheel drive shelf road.

DISTANCE: The round trip is 16 miles.

DIFFICULTY: Difficult. Moderate for six miles, then difficult on the two-mile shelf road to the top. You will need to push your bike in places, and riding back down the shelf road requires some technical skills.

RIDE TIME: Allow at least four hours.

CAUTION: Sunny skies can quickly degenerate to thunderstorms and snow at higher elevations, especially above 11,000 feet, even in mid summer. Essential equipment for this ride is a rain jacket with hood, rain pants and full-finger gloves.

The final few miles to the top of Argentine Pass are above timberline. If thunderheads in the area produce lightning, it's time to expeditiously make your way to lower and less exposed elevations.

MAPS: USGS 30 x 60 minute: Denver West; USGS 7.5 minute: Georgetown, Grays Peak, Montezuma.

THE ROUTE: The Argentine Pass toll road, completed in 1871, is the highest pass road ever built over the Continental Divide.

Constructed to provide contiguous thoroughfare to the gold and silver mines above Peru Creek, the route was cursed by the elements

for wagon passage on the narrow west approach. The west side is now open only to hikers, and recently mountain bikers, and is an optional addition to today's *RIDE GUIDE* route.

On the initial mile up the Argentine Pass Road, the route switches back several times before straightening out and proceeding southwest. Other roads intersect the pass road at the switchbacks and are not marked; to avoid confusion follow the steepest route until the road levels and straightens, a little more than a mile from the start.

Leavenworth Creek will be to your left as you make the sustained ascent to timberline. The climbing is gradual along the old railroad grade of the Argentine Central Railway. This narrow gauge railway was used to haul ore out from the Waldorf Mine. It also transported tourists to the mining settlement.

At about 6 miles the road emerges from the trees at the site of the old Waldorf Mine. The town of Waldorf stood alongside the mine complete with hotel, mill, machine shop and stables and boasted the highest post office in the country (11,666 feet).

The next two miles are rocky and steep. You will have to walk your bike as you traverse the 13,000 foot wall of rock that forms the Continental Divide, but the magnificent views from the top are well worth the energy spent getting there.

Horseshoe Basin and Peru Creek are to the west and below (once, best known for silver, and now for great mountain biking) and Grays and Torreys peaks are to the northwest; Argentine Peak is due south. Further to the west are the Tenmile and Gore ranges.

Bike Path to Cherry Creek Reservoir

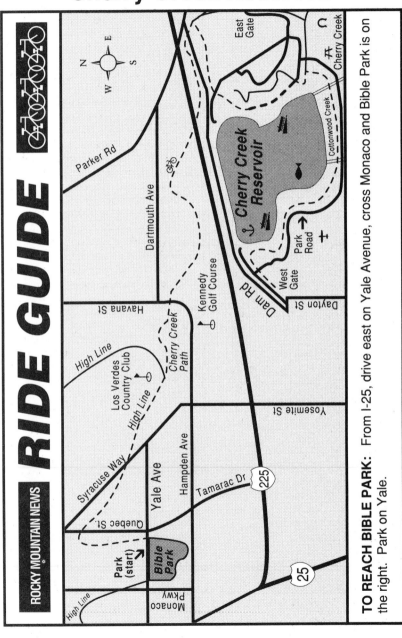

TO REACH BIBLE PARK: From I-25, drive east on Yale Avenue, cross Monaco and Bible Park is on the right. Park on Yale.

ROCKY MOUNTAIN NEWS **RIDE GUIDE**

BICYCLE: Road bike or mountain bike. However, if you plan to do any exploring on alternate routes, a fatter tired bike will be more comfortable and versatile.

SURFACE: Nearly the entire ride is on paved bike path. Some sections of the path around Cherry Creek Reservoir may be rough.

DISTANCE: Round trip, the route is about 22 miles.

DIFFICULTY: The ride is easy, with several little hills.

RIDE TIME: Plan on spending two hours or more to complete the route.

WILDLIFE: There are two prairie dog colonies along the route. The Cherry Creek State Recreation Area has a small herd of deer, coyotes, rabbits and many species of birds. Fishing in the reservoir is said to be excellent.

THE ROUTE: Start pedalling north on the High Line Canal bike path; you will find it across Yale Avenue from Bible Park near the intersection of Quebec Street. After about a half mile the path (and canal) will bend around to the southeast and parallel South Syracuse Way.

At about two and a half miles the path will intersect with the path to Cherry Creek Reservoir (follow the signs) at a prairie dog colony. Bear to the right and follow Cherry Creek for not quite a mile, until you dip under Havana Street and roll through the Kennedy Golf Course.

After scaling a short steep hill, take an immediate right (follow signs for Cherry Creek Reservoir), descend under I-225 and begin a half mile climb up to Parker Road.

Go right along Parker Road, cross Vaughn Way and look for the path into Cherry Creek Reservoir immediately on the right. The sidewalk adjacent to Parker Road is narrow, but you won't be on it long.

On the half mile descent into the park, the path crosses the park road and winds along the swim and water-ski beaches. A concessions facility is open during the warmer months.

For the next half mile follow the shore line on park roads and through the parking lots for the shade shelters and boat ramps. As you exit the last parking lot, you will find the path again on the right. Note that there may be some construction blocking the path at this point. In that case, use the park road (it's visible) until you can find the path again.

After crossing Cherry Creek at the southern most end of the reservoir, the path bends to the north past the nature study area, the model airplane field and the prairie dog colony. Finally, you will reach the west picnic area, where the path crosses the road and continues to the west gate.

Return the way you came. It is possible to ride the dam road (Crest Road) instead, but this is not recommended due to the very narrow shoulders.

MAPS: A map of Cherry Creek Reservoir is available at the East and West Gates, and it's free.

SHIFTING GEARS: Proper shoes for cycling make the pedalling more fun and efficient. Tennis type shoes feel alright for short distances, but after moderate mileage, you may find the pedals are nipping at your feet. Check your favorite bike shop for stiff-soled cycling shoes.

Chair Rocks

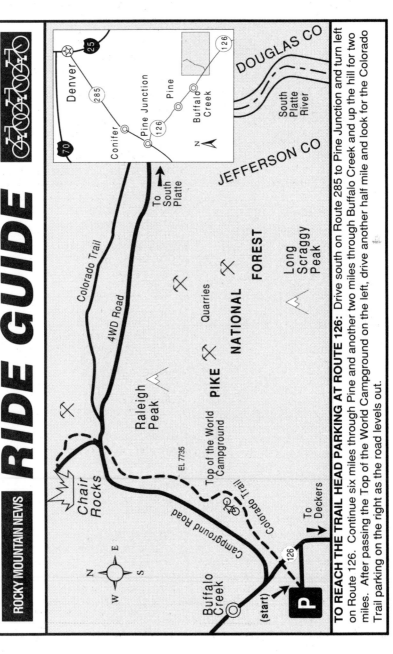

TO REACH THE TRAIL HEAD PARKING AT ROUTE 126: Drive south on Route 285 to Pine Junction and turn left on Route 126. Continue six miles through Pine and another two miles through Buffalo Creek and up the hill for two miles. After passing the Top of the World Campground on the left, drive another half mile and look for the Colorado Trail parking on the right as the road levels out.

ROCKY MOUNTAIN NEWS *RIDE GUIDE*

BICYCLE: Mountain bike with knobby tires.

SURFACE: This single track hiking trail has a mildly diversified surface for a bicycle. The trail changes from smooth and hard packed to loose dirt to slightly rocky, but it is very rideable.

DISTANCE: Round trip is about eight and a half miles.

DIFFICULTY: This ride is moderate. In several places you will need better than beginner mountain bike handling skills.

RIDE TIME: Allow about three hours to complete the ride.

THE ROUTE: The ride from Route 126 to Chair Rocks follows a four mile section of the 470 mile Colorado Trail. This recently completed, recreational single track offers some of the best off-road cycling available in close proximity to the Denver metro area.

Mountain bikes are welcome on the Colorado Trail, but as with any multi-use trail, please yield to hikers and equestrians, and don't ride off the path.

From the trail head parking lot, find the trail to the northeast and head back towards Route 126. Cross 126, ride down the embankment and pass through the fence at the trail sign.

The trail rolls along on its way to Chair Rocks without any sustained climbs or descents. The path is well defined, but swerves radically at times, so pay attention. Also, you will cut across several access roads to the old quarries that dotted this part of the Pike National Forest.

Initially, you will descend, level out and slowly climb as you traverse a ridge with a southeastern exposure. At about two miles there is a wonderful view of Long Scraggy Peak to the southeast and Pikes Peak to the south.

Continuing north, you'll pass through sections of the popular Top of the World campground. Don't be alarmed, but the campground attracts some ATV (vrroom vrroom) enthusiasts. They have their own trails and I won't comment further.

At about four miles the trail intersects a four wheel drive road. You will see the road has a branch that goes north and is dead ahead. Look off to the right of this branch and you'll pick up the trail once more. Note that this is no longer the Colorado Trail, and is not marked.

This quarter mile section dead ends at Chair Rocks. Be sure to take a break on the these huge rock outcroppings. The view to the west is magnificent. Look to the southwest for Windy Peak and The Castle.

SHIFTING GEARS: This and other parts of the Colorado Trail are open to dogs, and there is no formal leash law. I strongly recommend against taking your dog along on a bicycle outing.

I have seen some of the heartiest of our four legged pals reduced to palpitating blobs with very stiff limbs. It is easy to underestimate the speed and distance covered by mountain bikes on the trail.

Dogs are also a potential threat to the wildlife that inhabits our national forests.

Chatfield to Arrowhead

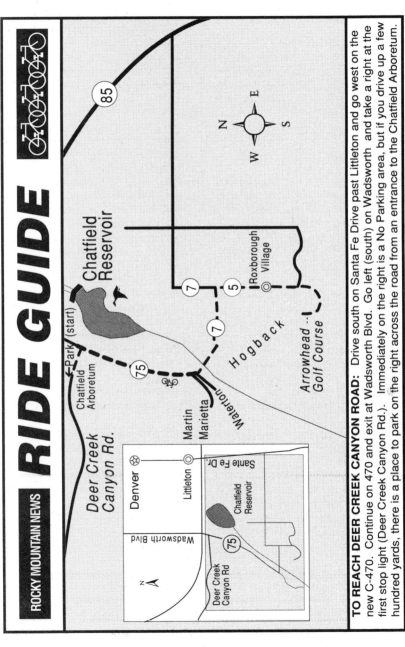

TO REACH DEER CREEK CANYON ROAD: Drive south on Santa Fe Drive past Littleton and go west on the new C-470. Continue on 470 and exit at Wadsworth Blvd. Go left (south) on Wadsworth and take a right at the first stop light (Deer Creek Canyon Rd.). Immediately on the right is a No Parking area, but if you drive up a few hundred yards, there is a place to park on the right across the road from an entrance to the Chatfield Arboretum.

ROCKY MOUNTAIN NEWS **RIDE GUIDE**

BICYCLE: The ride is better on a road bike, but a mountain bike will do.

SURFACE: Smooth, well maintained state and county roads. Route 75 has big wide shoulders, but you'll find them narrow on the Douglas County roads. In Spring, there will be some sand on the shoulders.

DISTANCE: Round trip will be approximately 20 miles.

DIFFICULTY: This ride is easy. There are several short climbs.

RIDE TIME: Allow at least two hours for the round trip.

THE ROUTE: From your parking place on Deer Creek Canyon Road, head back towards Chatfield and go right (south) on Route 75.

Although 75 is similar to an interstate (two lanes in each direction), it is not heavily traveled and has shoulders on which you can ride two abreast. This road has been a favorite training route for cyclists for years.

As you head south, you'll get a great view of Chatfield Reservoir. Keep one eye in the sky to catch sight of a Great Blue Heron, cruising from its rookery home in Chatfield. You won't mistake it for another bird; it will look about the size of a small bomber.

Four miles down the road take a left at the signs for Roxborough. You'll pass the entrance to Waterton Canyon on the right; if you're feeling additionally motivated, you may want to do a little exploring in the canyon.

In another mile and a half go right (south) at the intersection onto Douglas County Route 5. Continue on 5 through Roxborough Village, past the park entrance on the left, and into the Arrowhead Golf Course. The road bends to the right and there is a sign for the golf course, where you can take a break. A restaurant operates during the warmer months.

You have entered Hogback heaven, and the massive red rocks are worth checking out. Take a tour of this once, planned-to-be posh residential area.

On the return, scan a long stretch of hogback parallelling the foothills to the north. You'll also get a glimpse of the impressive Martin Marietta facility.

EXTRA: If you go bright and early on a Saturday or Sunday morning during the warmer months, you may see the sky over Chatfield dotted with colorful hot air balloons.

MAPS: Denver area road map or atlas. U.S. Forest Service: Pike National Forest.

SHIFTING GEARS: There are road tires available for mountain bikes (26 inch wheels) that will make your trailblazer much more like a road machine.

Switching from knobbies to slicks can be easier and faster (but unfortunately more expensive) by mounting the road tires on an extra set of wheels. With a wheel change, you'll never be more than minutes away from either pedalling on the dirt or the pavement.

Deer Creek Canyon

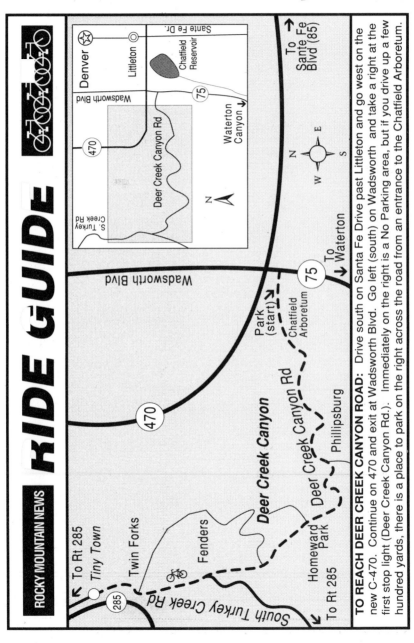

TO REACH DEER CREEK CANYON ROAD: Drive south on Santa Fe Drive past Littleton and go west on the new C-470. Continue on 470 and exit at Wadsworth Blvd. Go left (south) on Wadsworth and take a right at the first stop light (Deer Creek Canyon Rd.). Immediately on the right is a No Parking area, but if you drive up a few hundred yards, there is a place to park on the right across the road from an entrance to the Chatfield Arboretum.

ROCKY MOUNTAIN NEWS **RIDE GUIDE**

BICYCLE: Road bike or mountain bike.

SURFACE: The road surface in the canyon is generally good. However, there can be rough sections if we have had a snowy winter. In that case, also watch for sandy shoulders in the spring.

This road twists and turns its way to the top and the shoulders are narrow in places, so make an effort to stay as far right as possible.

DISTANCE: The round trip to Tiny Town and back to your car is about 24 miles.

DIFFICULTY: The ride is moderate to difficult, mostly because of the climb up Deer Creek Canyon, not the mileage.

RIDE TIME: Allow at least two hours or more to reach Tiny Town and return.

THE ROUTE: Deer Creek Canyon is a great place to prepare for riding the roads of the high country. It approximates many of the popular mountain passes that you may be planning to ride this summer, and it's easy to access from Denver. Also, it is generally rideable from early spring to late fall, so you can rely on the route when others are not rideable.

Head west on Deer Creek Canyon Road (Jefferson County 124) and begin the nine mile climb to the top of the canyon. As you start out, the Chatfield Arboretum is on the left

and then you'll pass the former Johns Manville Research Center on the right. The first few miles will roll along gaining only a little elevation.

In a mile or so you will start snaking your way through the canyon and the pedalling will become considerably harder. On the weekends, during better weather, look for rock climbers in the canyon. In some places, they may be just overhead.

At about six miles is Phillipsburg. On the left is South Deer Creek Road, a challenging mountain bike ride that ends up in Conifer.

The road continues to wind out of Phillipsburg for a mile to Homewood Park where it straightens out a bit. However, the grade becomes more severe for the final push over the saddle and down to Fenders.

At Fenders, go right at the T (the fire station is dead ahead) on South Turkey Creek Road and continue through Twin Forks to Tiny Town. The last two and a half miles to Tiny Town is a flowing descent where you can move right along.

There is a convenience store in Tiny Town where you can fuel up if necessary, and take a break before the return trip. You may also want to check out the mini hamlet from which this town gets its name.

If you are interested in pedalling more mileage in conjunction with riding Deer Creek Canyon, there are several ways to make a complete loop. Use regional road maps and Denver bike route maps to design your route.

Devils Head Loop

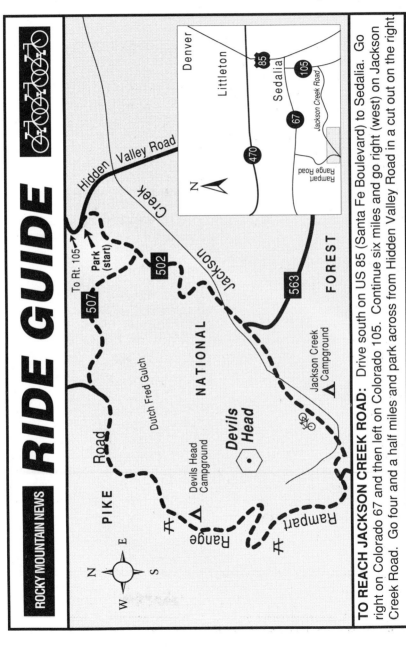

TO REACH JACKSON CREEK ROAD: Drive south on US 85 (Santa Fe Boulevard) to Sedalia. Go right on Colorado 67 and then left on Colorado 105. Continue six miles and go right (west) on Jackson Creek Road. Go four and a half miles and park across from Hidden Valley Road in a cut out on the right.

ROCKY MOUNTAIN NEWS **RIDE GUIDE**

BICYCLE: Mountain bike.

SURFACE: Smooth dirt roads. You may experience sections of loose dirt from spring grading, but the road should be firmly packed by summer's end.

DISTANCE: The loop is about 22 miles.

DIFFICULTY: This loop is moderately difficult. There is one sustained climb of about three miles and several shorter ascents.

RIDE TIME: Allow at least three hours.

MAPS: US Forest Service: Pike National Forest; USGS 30 x 60 minute: Bailey.

WILDLIFE: The area supports deer, elk, bear, wild turkeys and numerous other bird species.

THE ROUTE: The Rampart Range has long been a popular camping and hiking region of the Pike National Forest. The many Forest Routes that branch from the Rampart Range Road cut through incredibly rugged and rocky surroundings.

The massive, smooth rock formations along Jackson Creek are a rock climber's delight; they also provide a magnificent scenic backdrop. Because of the numerous aspen groves, Jackson Creek Road is a wonderful place to experience the colors of autumn.

From your parking place, head southwest on Jackson Creek Road; it will be marked as Forest Route 502.

At a half mile, you will pass the Jackson Volunteer Fire Department #105 to the right, and at about two miles the road forks; bear to the right.

For nearly the first three miles, the road climbs and bends to the intersection of Forest Route 507 on the right. You will have entered the Pike National Forest. The pine forest on the climb is pristine and beautiful.

Continue straight on 502 for a steep mile and a half descent into the canyon below. The road levels out at just over four miles and crosses Jackson Creek, then continues parallel to the creek, which is to the right.

For the next six miles you will pedal through tremendous rock formations. Very gradually, the route gains elevation.

At nearly six miles, Forest Route 563 joins on the left, and another mile farther you'll enter a peaceful meadow. This is a good place to take a break and check out the scenery. Look for Devils Head.

Jackson Creek Campground is at just over eight miles. Then, the road climbs more vertically to the Rampart Range Road at about mile 10.

Go right (north) on the Rampart Range Road and continue to gradually ascend for another three miles. After a half mile coast, the Devils Head Campground road is on the right. Follow the sign toward Sedalia.

The road rolls along and drops down to the intersection of Forest Route 507 about 17 miles into the trip. Go right and descend for three miles to rejoin route 502.

Take a left and enjoy the fast, three-mile twisting plummet back to your car.

Echo Lake via Juniper Pass

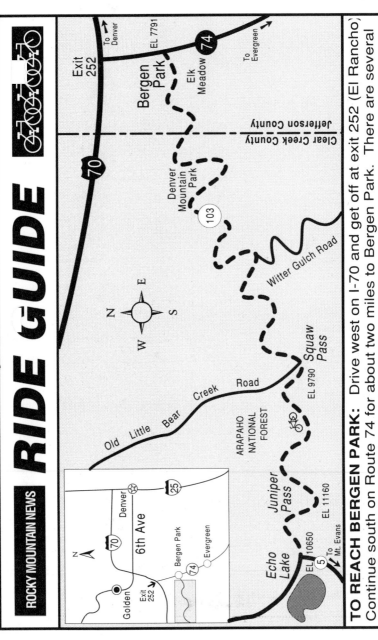

TO REACH BERGEN PARK: Drive west on I-70 and get off at exit 252 (El Rancho). Continue south on Route 74 for about two miles to Bergen Park. There are several lots in which to park.

ROCKY MOUNTAIN NEWS *RIDE GUIDE*

BICYCLE: Road Bike or mountain bike with road tires.

SURFACE: Colorado Route 103 is smooth and in good condition. There are some rough spots for the first few miles out of Bergen Park; make note for the descent on the return trip.

DISTANCE: The round trip is 36 miles.

DIFFICULTY: Moderate to difficult. The mileage is not devastating, but the first 16 miles of pedalling are uphill, over an average grade of around 4%. You'll gain nearly 3400 vertical feet on this climb.

RIDE TIME: Allow at least three hours to complete the route.

THE ROUTE: This ride over Squaw and Juniper Pass is a beautiful route with extraordinary views. Plan on making several stops on the climb to check out the scenery; you will probably want to rest your legs as well on this relatively long escalation.

Head west on Squaw Pass Road, Colorado 103, toward Echo Lake (it's well marked). Forthwith, you will begin your ascent into the high country.

On your left (south), in a lovely meadow are several very old barns that frequently appear on postcards. Just beyond is Bergen Peak, which is accessible from Elk Meadow, one of the Jefferson County Open Space facilities.

After a little more than two miles you will enter Clear Creek County. For several miles, the road winds through one of the many, and relatively unknown, Denver Mountain Parks.

At about seven miles, Witter

Gulch Road is on the left, and a couple of miles further you'll crest Squaw Pass. You may not recognize the pass (it's not well marked) except that there's a picnic area, and Old Little Bear Creek Road is on the right.

Don't relax here because the road will continue to rise for the next seven miles to Juniper Pass.

There is plenty of captivating scenery to keep your mind off the work load. At about 14 miles, find Virginia Canyon rising above Idaho Springs to the north. You can't actually see Idaho Springs, but you'll see the remains of the many old mines that dot the hills of this area.

Look again to locate the "Oh-My-God Road" snaking from mine shaft to mine shaft on its route to Central City. This road is a wonderful Fall and Winter mountain bike route and will be featured in a future *RIDE GUIDE.*

After rolling over Juniper Pass, watch for the incredible view to the south. Here, you will get a distinct feeling for the altitude gained on the trip up. The Mount Evans Wilderness area unfolds far below.

A two mile coast will then put you at the Echo Lake lodge, where you can relax and buy food and beverage.

After the short climb back to Juniper Pass, the remainder of the return trip is a relatively fast descent, if you hadn't guessed. Be extra careful of the auto traffic on weekends during the summer; drivers may be concentrating on the view rather than the road.

If possible, I recommend that you conquer this route on a weekday. On a recent weekday trip, there were so few cars that Rocket Rod and I rode side by side in many places. Conversation is a good distraction when pedalling uphill.

Elk Meadow

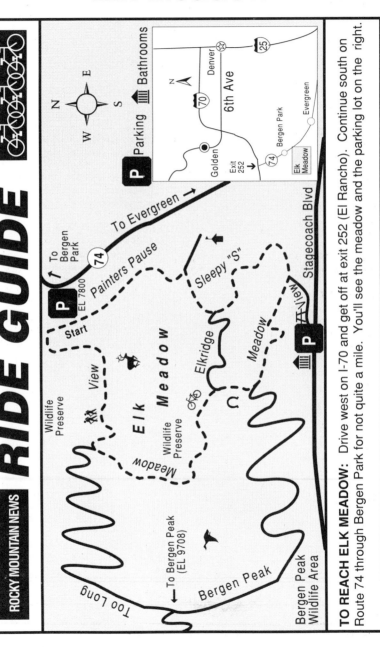

ROCKY MOUNTAIN NEWS *RIDE GUIDE*

Wildlife Preserve

Too Long

To Bergen Peak (EL 9708)

Bergen Peak

Bergen Peak Wildlife Area

Elk Meadow

Wildlife Preserve

View

Start

EL 7800

Painters Pause

To Bergen Park

74

To Evergreen

Sleepy "S"

Elkridge

Meadow

A-View

Stagecoach Blvd

P Parking ▥ Bathrooms

N E W S

Denver

25

70

6th Ave

Golden

Exit 252

Bergen Park

Evergreen

74

Elk Meadow

TO REACH ELK MEADOW: Drive west on I-70 and get off at exit 252 (El Rancho). Continue south on Route 74 through Bergen Park for not quite a mile. You'll see the meadow and the parking lot on the right.

ROCKY MOUNTAIN NEWS **RIDE GUIDE**

BICYCLE: This is a mountain bike ride. Knobby tires are preferable, especially if you plan to venture up the Bergen Peak or Too Long Trails.

SURFACE: Smooth, single track trails are well maintained.

DISTANCE: This loop is about five miles. There are additional trails for increased difficulty and more mileage.

DIFFICULTY: Easy to moderate. If you choose to ride the Too Long or Bergen Peak trails, then the riding is difficult.

RIDE TIME: Allow at least an hour and a half.

WILDLIFE: Elk Meadow supports a variety of wildlife including elk, deer, porcupines and many species of birds. On Bergen Peak one day, I watched a Bald Eagle soar overhead for nearly 30 minutes. On another outing, as a fire engine on Colorado 74 sped by with siren blaring, a family of young coyotes howled furiously from their den, just off the trail.

THE ROUTE: Elk Meadow is my favorite of all the wonderful Jefferson County Open Space facilities. The park offers outdoor entertainment for the whole family. If only some of your group are mountain bikers, the others will enjoy hiking or picnicking while you take a ride. From the parking lot, access the park through the gate and go left (south) on the Painters Pause Trail. You will coast down this gradual descent for one mile to the intersection of the Sleepy "S" where you take a right. On the Painters Pause there are bar checks (logs) every so often to help eliminate trail erosion. Don't ride off the trail and around them as that will defeat their purpose.

The Sleepy "S" bends and climbs for just over a mile; you will pass the Elkridge Trail on the right on the way to the intersection of the Meadow Trail.

Go right on the Meadow Trail and gradually climb, switching back several times, up past the Bergen Peak Trail intersection on the left. (The Bergen Peak Trail ascends to the summit of Bergen Peak, the high point in the park. It's scenic, but strenuous riding and will be featured in a future *RIDE GUIDE*.)

Back on the Meadow Trail, a quarter mile ahead, the trail levels out then forks. Continuing to the left at the fork, the next mile rolls through the trees, crosses several streams and breaks out into the meadow.

Gliding by the Too Long Trail (which also climbs steeply to Bergen Peak) on the left, the final descent is about a mile back to the parking lot.

SHIFTING GEARS: It is important for cyclists to adhere to several simple rules when riding in Elk Meadow or on any other mountain trails: Stay on the trails, don't cut or lock up your tires on the switchbacks, and yield to horses. You might also thank hikers when they yield to let you cruise by. Note that, at one time, Jefferson County Open Space officials were considering banning bikes from the parks. Don't give mountain bikers a bad name; I would hate to see us lose such beautiful places to ride.

Farris Creek Loop

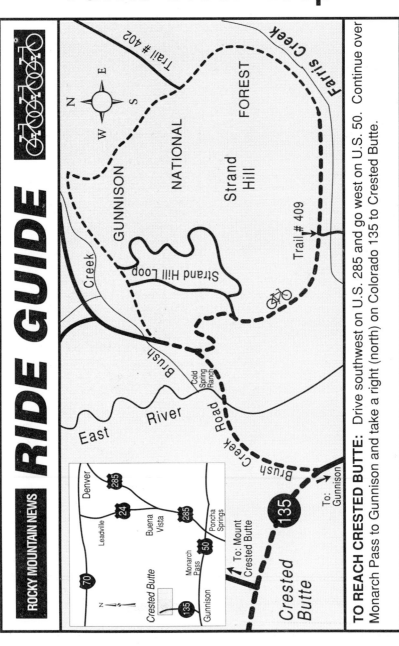

ROCKY MOUNTAIN NEWS

RIDE GUIDE

TO REACH CRESTED BUTTE: Drive southwest on U.S. 285 and go west on U.S. 50. Continue over Monarch Pass to Gunnison and take a right (north) on Colorado 135 to Crested Butte.

ROCKY MOUNTAIN NEWS *RIDE GUIDE*

BICYCLE: Mountain bike.

SURFACE: The loop starts and ends on paved county roads, but includes smooth dirt roads, four wheel drive roads and single track trails. There are several rocky sections of single track.

DISTANCE: The loop is about 20 miles.

DIFFICULTY: This ride is moderately difficult with several short steep climbs and one technical descent.

RIDE TIME: Allow at least three hours.

WILDFLOWERS: Wildflowers abound in the mountains around Crested Butte and are one of the many highlights of summer trail riding in this area. Stop and enjoy the "Sound of Music" serenity of these alpine gardens.

MAPS: Paradise Bikes, Crested Butte: The Pathfinders Trail Map; USGS 7.5 minute: Crested Butte, Gothic, Pearl Pass.

THE ROUTE: Crested Butte emerged a decade ago as the premier area in the world for off-road cycling. At that time, there wasn't much competition; mountain biking, for the most part, was invented and developed in Crested Butte.

Today, the original mountain biking hamlet is still considered nirvana to fat tire pedallers. A system of high country routes has been mapped and marked allowing more riding time and less time looking at a compass.

It's easy to agree with locals when they say "Crested Butte is the mountain bike capital of the world."

Local off-road aficionado Ralph Marra made certain I didn't miss any of the great scenery along Farris Creek Loop.

From Crested Butte, head out of town towards Gunnison on Colorado 135. Go left on Brush Creek Road at two miles (there's a sign for the airport).

Continue about three and a half miles to the trail head (it's marked) and go right. You'll cross the East River and pass Cold Spring Ranch to the left about three quarters of a mile before the trail head.

The surface becomes slightly rocky (four wheel drive road) on a stiff one mile climb. At the top of the hill the Strand Hill Trail intersects on your left.

Pass through a fence another half mile further and roll on down into the valley following the old road. Double Top is above and dead ahead.

With # 409 converging on the right, the trail begins to bend to the north and meets Trail # 402 about one more mile ahead.

The valley becomes the home of several hunting camps during that season (Autumn). In mid-summer, you may encounter an obstacle course of cows grazing there, but it will just add to your adventure.

The next mile gradually climbs to a cattle fence. Beyond is a great view of Teocalli Mountain, and the West Brush Creek drainage.

Prepare for a steep, rocky and technical descent off the hill. At the bottom (about a mile) look for the sign, To Canal, and take a left.

Advance two miles to the canal; you'll pass the back side of the Strand Hill Trail on the way.

Ford the canal and go left on the Brush Creek Road and back to town.

Foothills Panorama

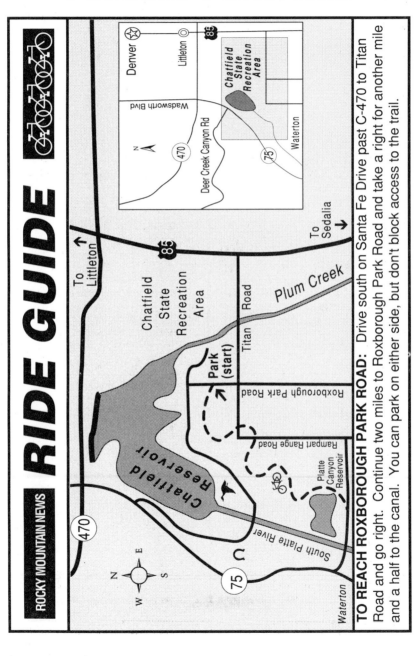

TO REACH ROXBOROUGH PARK ROAD: Drive south on Santa Fe Drive past C-470 to Titan Road and go right. Continue two miles to Roxborough Park Road and take a right for another mile and a half to the canal. You can park on either side, but don't block access to the trail.

ROCKY MOUNTAIN NEWS *RIDE GUIDE*

BICYCLE: Mountain bike or fatter tire style bicycle.

SURFACE: This section of the High Line Canal trail has a relatively smooth dirt surface, with an occasional, mildly rutted section. Make a concerted effort not to stray off the path, as the dreaded Tribulus Terrestris, the weed that produces the killer bull thorn, may be lurking in wait of your tires on the sides of the trail.

DISTANCE: The round trip is about 11 miles.

DIFFICULTY: This pedaling is easy. The ride can be enjoyed by the entire family.

RIDE TIME: Allow at least an hour and a half to go down and back.

THE ROUTE: The trail follows the southernmost section of the High Line Canal, while cutting through some beautiful Front Range horse country.

The High Line Canal was completed in 1883 by the British-owned Northern Colorado Irrigation Company. A gravity canal, it was built to irrigate some 20,000 acres of crop land at a cost of $650,000.

Today, water is run in the canal from the South Platte River, only when surplus water (mostly runoff) is available and when water is needed.

Head west from your parking place and follow the trail as it bends to the south. You will have an exceptional view of the Foothills all the way south to Waterton.

At about a mile, the trail meanders through a rural residential area. Another half mile or so further, you will cut through a picturesque horse farm.

Continuing through horse country, the route crosses Titan Road and soon thereafter Rampart Range Road. You will, no doubt, encounter equestrians on your ride. Make sure to yield to them. To some horses, a man on a bike is as a red flag to a bull.

The final zigzag takes you around Platte Canyon Reservoir and ends at Waterton Road.

Before you return, you may want to check out the Kassler Water Treatment Plant or ride into Waterton Canyon, just up the road a few hundred yards to the right.

On the return trip, the Hogback is well defined, running north as far as the eye can follow. A great view of the Denver skyline sitting above Chatfield Reservoir can be had on the final mile back to the car.

ARBOREAL TRIVIA: You can't miss the large cottonwood and elm trees that line the canal. Recently, the Colorado State Forest Service took an inventory along the entire High Line Canal that accounted for 18,869 trees.

An effort is being made to put together a management program for the care of trees on the canal. Disease has taken its toll.

MAPS: Colorado State Parks: Urban Trails in Colorado-Denver Metro Area.

Georgia Pass - Part One

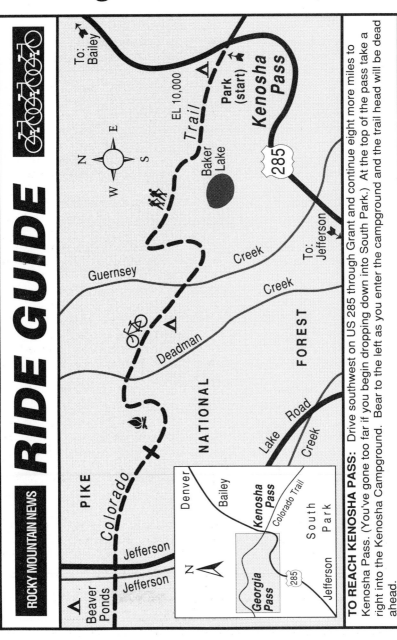

TO REACH KENOSHA PASS: Drive southwest on US 285 through Grant and continue eight more miles to Kenosha Pass. (You've gone too far if you begin dropping down into South Park.) At the top of the pass take a right into the Kenosha Campground. Bear to the left as you enter the campground and the trail head will be dead ahead.

ROCKY MOUNTAIN NEWS *RIDE GUIDE*

BICYCLE: Mountain bike.

SURFACE: Smooth single track hiking trail. There are very occasional rocks, roots and stumps; this trail is the ultimate rideable single track.

DISTANCE: The round trip is about 24 miles.

DIFFICULTY: The ride is between moderate and difficult. Even though the mileage is not overly long nor the climbing severe, 24 miles of single track riding at altitude can be a workout. The route gains about a half mile vertically over the 24 miles.

RIDE TIME: Allow at least five hours for the round trip.

SCENIC QUALITY: The trail cuts through diverse terrain including aspen groves, beautiful pine forests, meadows covered with wildflowers and magnificent views of mountain and plain.

The ride is sensational in the Fall (before late September or early October) when the aspens change.

MAPS: Colorado Trail Map ; USGS 7.5 minute: Jefferson, Boreas Pass; US Forest Service: Pike National Forest.

THE ROUTE: This ride has been divided into two parts, the first half featured this week and the last half next, in order to provide all of the details.

The Colorado Trail offers some of the very best mountain biking in the state, and the section between Kenosha Pass and Georgia Pass is a prime example.

From the trailhead, you will start out gradually climbing to the northwest through a lovely aspen grove. After nearly a mile you'll crest a ridge and South Park unfolds to the southwest framed by the peaks of the Continental Divide. The little town of Jefferson is just below.

The next mile and a half descends into the park alternating through aspens then meadows filled with lupines, daisies and paintbrush. On the descent there is a good view of Mount Guyot to the west. Georgia Pass is just to the north of Guyot.

The Colorado Trail is extremely well marked with trail markers on trees, but in the open meadows you will need to follow posts and rock cairins.

At about three miles the trail crosses Guernsey Creek. A half mile further, you will parallel another small creek for a few hundred yards then jog through it to the right. Groups of branches across the trail will help to direct you here and in several other locations.

Winding up a short hill, cross a Forest Road, then soon after splash into Deadman Creek. If you want to avoid the possibility of getting wet (boo!) there's a log crossing in the woods to the left.

At almost five miles, merge into an old road and follow it for a few hundred yards, cross a culvert and pick up the trail again immediately on the left.

Notice that you are in forest that totally burned about ten years ago. The regrowth of aspens and pines is well underway; when I first rode here five years ago, the area looked devastated.

Pass through a gate (make sure to close it) several tenths of a mile beyond and descend to Jefferson Lake Road at about six miles.

Georgia Pass - Part Two

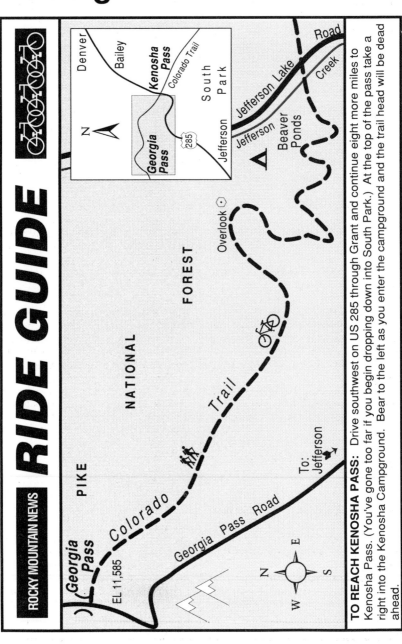

ROCKY MOUNTAIN NEWS

RIDE GUIDE

Inset map:
N

Denver

Bailey

Kenosha Pass

Colorado Trail

South Park

285

Jefferson

Georgia Pass

Main map:
Road

Jefferson Lake

Creek

Jefferson

Beaver Ponds

Overlook ⊙

FOREST

NATIONAL

Colorado Trail

PIKE

Georgia Pass

EL 11,585

Georgia Pass Road

To: Jefferson

N E S W

TO REACH KENOSHA PASS: Drive southwest on US 285 through Grant and continue eight more miles to Kenosha Pass. (You've gone too far if you begin dropping down into South Park.) At the top of the pass take a right into the Kenosha Campground. Bear to the left as you enter the campground and the trail head will be dead ahead.

BICYCLE: Mountain bike.

SURFACE: Smooth, single- track hiking trail. There are very occasional rocks, roots and stumps; this trail is the ultimate rideable single track.

DISTANCE: The round trip is about 24 miles.

DIFFICULTY: The ride is between moderate and difficult. Even though the mileage is not overly long nor the climbing severe, 24 miles of single- track riding at altitude can be a workout. The route gains about a half mile vertically over the 24 miles.

RIDE TIME: Allow at least five hours for the round trip.

SCENIC QUALITY: The trail cuts through diverse terrain including aspen groves, beautiful pine forests, meadows covered with wildflowers and magnificent views of mountain and plain.

The ride is sensational in the Fall (late September and early October) when the aspens change.

MAPS: Colorado Trail Map; USGS 7.5 minute: Jefferson, Boreas Pass; U.S. Forest Service: Pike National Forest.

THE ROUTE: This ride has been divided into two parts, the first half featured last week and the last half this week, in order to provide all the details.

Before continuing west from the Jefferson Lake Road trailhead of the Colorado Trail, check out the beaver ponds 100 yards up the road to the north.

Back on the trail, you will cross over Jefferson Creek and begin the gradual but steady climbing to the pass.

The trail will occasionally merge with and follow old forest roads. Keep an eye out for markers (posts and cairns of rocks).

On the climb to timberline, you'll be riding in beautiful pine forest with a bed of pine needles under the tires making for a soft and quiet surface.

At about seven and a half miles (from Kenosha Pass), the trail switches back and climbs a bit more steeply. And at slightly over eight miles, it begins to bend back to the west at a large rock formation (Lunch Rock). This is a great spot to take a break, have something to eat and check out the view from on top of the rocks. To the north are Jefferson Lake and Glacier and Whale peaks.

The final four-mile traverse takes you along a ridge above the Ohler Gulch drainage. The trail maintains a constant but gradual climb to the northwest.

At about ten and a half miles you'll reach timberline and a wildflower-filled basin. Mount Guyot and Bald Mountain are slightly to your left.

A mile further, the trail all but disappears in favor of alpine tundra. Massive rock cairns will guide you. Be prepared to push up the last few hundred yards to the Georgia Pass Road as the grade intensifies.

Once you reach the road, ride back to the left and look for markers on your right. There are sensational views into the Arapaho National Forest from the saddle on the north side of the road.

On the return trip, there are some fast descents on sections of the trail that are very closely lined with trees; stay under control.

Golden Gate Canyon

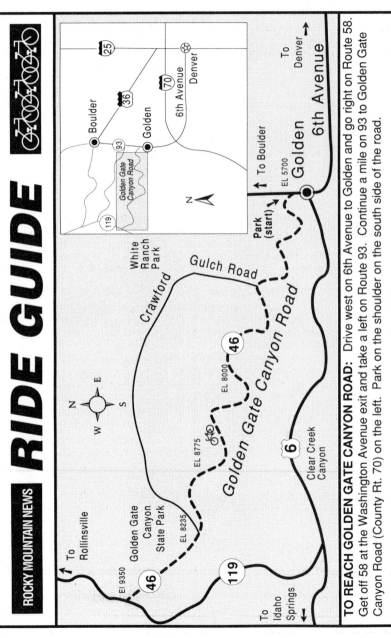

RIDE GUIDE

ROCKY MOUNTAIN NEWS

TO REACH GOLDEN GATE CANYON ROAD: Drive west on 6th Avenue to Golden and go right on Route 58. Get off 58 at the Washington Avenue exit and take a left on Route 93. Continue a mile on 93 to Golden Gate Canyon Road (County Rt. 70) on the left. Park on the shoulder on the south side of the road.

ROCKY MOUNTAIN NEWS *RIDE GUIDE*

BICYCLE: Road bike with appropriate mountain gearing, or mountain bike with road tires.

SURFACE: This route is on well maintained county roads. Watch for rough sections of pavement and sandy shoulders in the spring.

DISTANCE: From Golden, the round trip is about 34 miles.

DIFFICULTY: This ride is difficult and should be attempted only by cyclists in decent riding condition. The vertical gain over the 34 miles is nearly a mile and a half, with several sustained, steep grades and fast descents.

RIDE TIME: Allow at least three hours for the round trip.

THE ROUTE: I think of Golden Gate Canyon Road as the ideal Front Range fitness barometer for cyclists planning to participate in one of the recreational tours or century rides scheduled during the summer. The mileage is not overwhelming, but the three climbs going out and two coming back will tell you how you're going to do in the high country. If you complete this route to your satisfaction, you are probably ready for almost any hill in the state.

From your parking place, pedal west on Golden Gate Canyon Road and immediately begin the first of the three climbs to Route 119. Twisting through the canyon, you will pass Crawford Gulch Road on the right at about four miles and crest the first ascent near Guy Hill at seven miles. Catch your breath on a fast half mile coast before you

begin the next assault.

Over the next five miles, the grade is yet steeper than before and finally ends with another quick descent to the entrance of Golden Gate Canyon State Park on the right. Take a break at the Visitors Center if necessary; you've got one more healthy climb to Route 119.

The last five miles takes you along Ralston Creek and through the southernmost part of the park. You will likely spot some anglers in the creek or beside Kriley Pond on the right. The beautiful scenery will help take your mind off the final push to the intersection of 119.

For the record, Golden Gate Canyon Road was used as part of the route for the Coors Classic's Boulder Mountain Road Race in 1986, and for the Golden to Estes Park stage in 1987. You will be riding the same miles covered by many of the greatest bicycle racers in the world. That should make you feel better about the accomplishment.

If you desire mileage as well as the climbing, continue north on Route 119 through Rollinsville and take a right on Route 72. There's another good climb up to Wondervu and a very fast descent through Coal Creek Canyon to Route 93. Go right (south) and back to your car at Golden Gate Canyon Road on the right.

Otherwise, turn around and retrace your tracks. Don't forget to take plenty of water, at least two bottles.

MAPS: Regional road atlas or map; USGS 7.5 Minute Golden, Ralston Buttes, and Black Hawk.

Jim Creek Loop

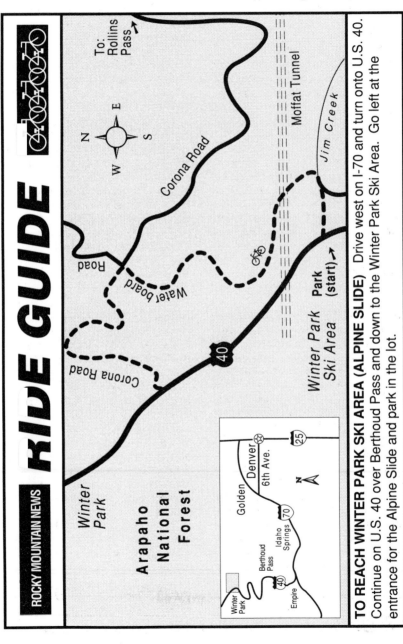

TO REACH WINTER PARK SKI AREA (ALPINE SLIDE) Drive west on I-70 and turn onto U.S. 40. Continue on U.S. 40 over Berthoud Pass and down to the Winter Park Ski Area. Go left at the entrance for the Alpine Slide and park in the lot.

ROCKY MOUNTAIN NEWS *RIDE GUIDE*

BICYCLE: Mountain bike.

SURFACE: On this loop, you will ride one short but slightly rocky section of trail, and then a smooth gravel road followed by the smooth shoulder of U.S. 40.

DISTANCE: Approximately nine and a half miles.

DIFFICULTY: This ride is easy; there is a gradual elevation gain of about 500 vertical feet to the highest point, and a slightly steeper, winding descent.

RIDE TIME: Allow an hour and a half or more.

THE ROUTE: High society is flourishing in the Winter Park area. Socialites aren't dressing up for fancy parties, but rather taking to the high country trails on their mountain bikes as prescribed by the Winter Park Fat Tire Society, known as FATS.

FATS has developed a system of over 200 miles of marked trails that coil through the Arapaho National Forest around Winter Park. These trails are designed to accommodate mountain bikers of a broad range of abilities and fitness levels.

The Jim Creek Loop serves as an excellent route for introducing the world off off-road bicycling. Many of the elements that make mountain biking in the back country so rewarding exist on this ride. Tour guides Greg Foley and Rob Jacobs of Fat Tire Tours provided highlights on a recent outing on the trail system.

From your parking place, the trail is just to the south (right) just across U.S. 40. After carefully crossing the highway, head east on the trail for about a mile.

The first mile is a little rocky and climbs a bit, but the Waterboard Road ahead is smooth and wide. Go left on the Waterboard Road at the aqueduct; you can't miss it.

When the aqueduct disappears underground to your right, you will be pedalling over the Moffat Tunnel. This railroad tunnel replaced the Corona Road, which was the old railroad bed for the Denver and Rio Grande Western railroad, and was the access over the continental divide via Rollins Pass. (A ride to the summit of Rollins Pass will be featured in the *RIDE GUIDE* later this summer.)

The road climbs gradually for the next two miles, then a little steeper to the intersection of the Corona Road. This is the highest point on the ride.

Go left on the Corona Road and through Arrow on the meandering descent down to U.S. 40. There are a number of blind corners on Corona Road. Be alert for auto traffic on the road, especially on weekends during the summer visitor season.

Go left on U.S. 40 and ride the paved shoulder a mile and a half back to the ski area and your car.

MAPS: Winter Park Fat Tire Society: Mountain Bike Trail System.

SHIFTING GEARS: For better traction and a more comfortable ride on dirt surfaces, let some air out of your tires. Most mountain bike tires have a range of recommended tire pressures listed on the sidewall. Generally, the rougher the riding surface, the less pressure you should have in your tires. Don't deflate them too much or you risk damaging both the tires and the rims.

Kerr Gulch Loop

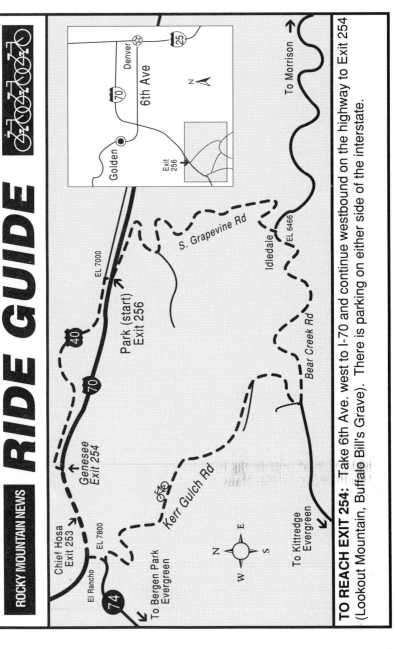

TO REACH EXIT 254: Take 6th Ave. west to I-70 and continue westbound on the highway to Exit 254 (Lookout Mountain, Buffalo Bill's Grave). There is parking on either side of the interstate.

ROCKY MOUNTAIN NEWS **RIDE GUIDE**

BICYCLE: This is a mountain bike ride.

SURFACE: The loop is completed on several surfaces including well maintained dirt roads, good county roads and a short section of I-70. The shoulders on the paved surfaces range from slightly narrow on Bear Creek Road to huge on I-70.

DISTANCE: The loop is approximately 18 miles.

DIFFICULTY: Moderate. There are some short, relatively steep climbs. The route gains about 1300 vertical feet, gradually, from Idledale to Route 74.

RIDE TIME: From an hour and a half to three hours.

THE ROUTE: On this ride you will experience interesting Foothills terrain that will keep both your eyes and your legs busy. The surface changes from pavement to dirt to pavement, several times.

Start riding south on South Grapevine Road (eastbound side of I-70). You'll descend a short hill, bend around to the right and begin a one mile climb. Bear left at the fork at about a half mile and follow South Grapevine for another three miles to Bear Creek Road The descent is fast; keep a lookout for an occasional auto. Also, in early spring, icy spots may exist.

Back on the pavement, wind your way west (right turn) on Bear Creek for three and a half miles and look for Kerr Gulch Road on the right. As you start up the rise (back on dirt) on Kerr Gulch, stay right. The road bends around to the left, goes down a short hill and forks. Steer to the right and begin a gradual five mile climb to Route 74.

There are some beautiful ranches and homes along Kerr Gulch Road, and the scenery is placid. I usually pass more dogs than autos.

The last half mile climbs steeply to Route 74 (back on pavement) where you turn right and descend to I-70. Merge onto the highway and exit again at the second opportunity, Exit 254 (Genesse). Cross over the highway and go right on Route 40 for a fast two mile coast back to Exit 256 and your car.

This is a particularly good cold weather bike ride. Both dirt roads, South Grapevine and Kerr Gulch are well plowed and stay relatively dry throughout the winter. Of course, use good judgement if it has recently snowed. In the Spring, however, you may encounter some muddy sections, especially on South Grapevine.

REMEMBER: For food or bathrooms try the town of Kittredge or the store across the street from El Rancho.

MAPS: Denver area regional road map or atlas; U.S.G.S.: 30 X 60 minute Denver West; U.S. Forest Service: Arapahoe National Forest.

SHIFTING GEARS: Riding a bicycle on the interstate is intimidating to some cyclists. In many respects riding on I-70 is safer than other roads, but you should always use a degree of caution, especially entering and exiting. Yield to autos that are entering or exiting as well. Keep in mind that bicycles are only permitted on specified sections of I-70.

Meridian International

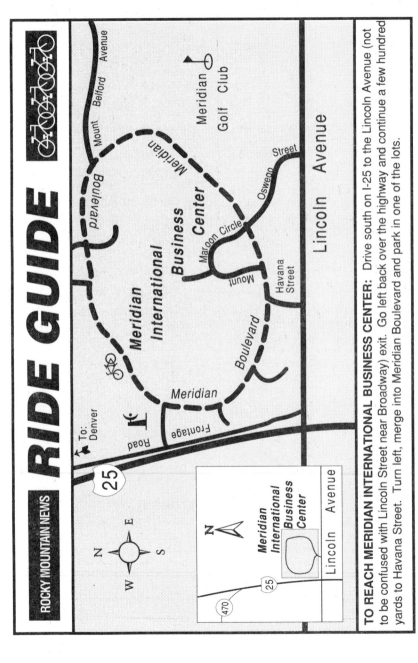

TO REACH MERIDIAN INTERNATIONAL BUSINESS CENTER: Drive south on I-25 to the Lincoln Avenue (not to be confused with Lincoln Street near Broadway) exit. Go left back over the highway and continue a few hundred yards to Havana Street. Turn left, merge into Meridian Boulevard and park in one of the lots.

ROCKY MOUNTAIN NEWS ***RIDE GUIDE***

BICYCLE: Road bike; this short circuit is a great place to stretch your legs on a lightweight cruiser.

SURFACE: Polished, silky smooth county road. Two full lanes in both directions circumscribe the center, divided by a large grassy median.

DISTANCE: A complete revolution is about two and one quarter miles.

DIFFICULTY: The loop is easy, but it's not flat. The more laps you do, the harder it gets.

RIDE TIME: Figure either side of ten minutes per cycle, depending on average speed.

FOR THE RECORD: Today's *RIDE GUIDE* was inspired largely by the controversy over closing to cyclists (and others) certain sections of roadway in Washington Park

Let's face it, Washington Park has been a multi-use recreational time bomb for years. And the thought, under any circumstances, that a mix of runners, walkers, wheelchairs, baby carriages, dogs on leashes, cars and speeding cyclists, sharing the same unrestricted roadway, will blend harmoniously is ridiculous.

Once the bomb has been defused then I'll recommend Washington Park as a wonderful place to ride your bike, leisurely with your family and friends.

The point is, there are many other better places to ride for exercise, but you're probably going to have to make a bit more effort to get to them.

THE ROUTE: Meridian International Business Center is a prime example of a sensational short circuit devoid of the many hazards that exist in city parks.

This "office park" is owned by British and American concerns and clearly illustrates that a carefully planned and maintained business environment can also be aesthetically pleasing. This is especially true if you're a cyclist.

Head east on Meridian Boulevard from your parking spot and descend a small hill and cross Oswego Street. The boulevard has two lanes traveling each direction for the entire loop, separated by a grassy median with trees and flowers and ponds. Autos won't have any trouble getting around you as long as you are riding in the right hand lane.

Meridian management is concerned that because there is so little auto traffic (recently, three cars overtook me in the course of an hour), cyclists tend to forget that they must abide by the rules, namely the state laws. This should not be a problem.

As the road bends to the north, you will pedal by Meridian Golf Club, a Jack Nicklaus designed course. Climbing very gradually, the route veers and descends to the west. Glance up for a nice view of the Front Range.

Twisting south then back to the east, there is one short and not too steep climb past Havana Street to conclude the lap.

Continue for as many loops as you can handle. By pushing, you will find that it won't take long to develop a little sweat on your brow.

Meridian is a great place to ride in the evening after work. The business center management has a very positive attitude about cyclists using the facility, but they are concerned about safety. On Tuesday evenings, there sometimes have been upwards of 100 riders; that's when you'll need to be especially careful. You may want to choose another day.

Mill Creek Road

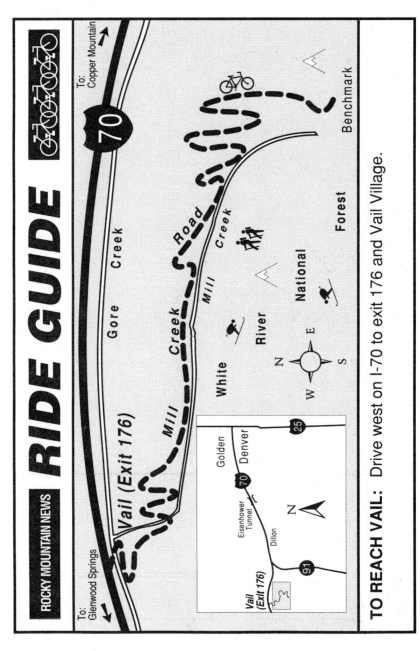

TO REACH VAIL: Drive west on I-70 to exit 176 and Vail Village.

ROCKY MOUNTAIN NEWS *RIDE GUIDE*

BICYCLE: Mountain Bike.

SURFACE: The route becomes gradually rougher, changing from smooth dirt to dirt to four-wheel drive road.

DISTANCE: To the top and back is about 20 miles.

DIFFICULTY: Moderate to difficult. This ride approaches the difficult category mostly because of the sustained climbing. The grades are not overly steep, except for several short portions near the top. Rocky sections of road contribute to effort made during the ascent.

RIDE TIME: Allow at least three and a half hours.

GREAT VIEWS: Sensational 360 degree view at the top includes the Gore Range, Eagles Nest Wilderness Area, the Sawatch Range, and the Holy Cross Wilderness Area.

MAPS: U.S. Forest Service: White River National Forest.

THE ROUTE: Vail is known world wide for superb skiing, and now the word is out about the great mountain biking there.

Skiing and mountain biking are recreational activities that can co-exist, each in its season, on the same terrain. Vail has successfully developed this concept by making some of the trails and service roads available to bikes.

Further, for those not interested in grunting their way up, the Lionshead Gondola will deposit you and your bike at Eagle's Nest. Then, test your skills in the terrain park (an observed trials type obstacle course), pick a trail and coast down.

Mountain bike purists have been riding up the mountain for years. Mill Creek Road has long been a popular route to access the higher elevations and the trails and bowls on the backside. The road gains about 3,000 vertical feet over the ten-mile climb to Benchmark.

From town, head south on Vail Road, cross Gore Creek and continue until the road turns to dirt; you'll pass through a gate on the way. This service road has recently been dubbed the Village Trail.

The trail switches back several times as you climb out of town. The surface here is relatively smooth and the grade gentle.

Pass under the Vista Bahn chairlift and continue another mile and a half to the intersection of the Mill Creek Road on your left; it's about four miles from town.

The surface changes from smooth to slightly rocky and the grade stiffens as you proceed up along Mill Creek. The road switches back to the north at about seven miles and you'll pass through an open gate. Stop to take in the wonderful view looking back across the valley at the Gore Range and at the road below.

At about nine miles the road crests a ridge, and a vista with Vail and Shrine Passes to the east is achieved.

There is steeper and rockier riding for the final thrust to Benchmark at the top. The view of the China Wall, the back bowls and the Sawatch Range make the pedaling time well spent. Locate the Mount of the Holy Cross to the southwest.

Either return the way you came, or link Benchmark with the top of the ski area on a single track spanning the China Wall; then ride one of the service road routes to the bottom.

Morgul-Bismarck

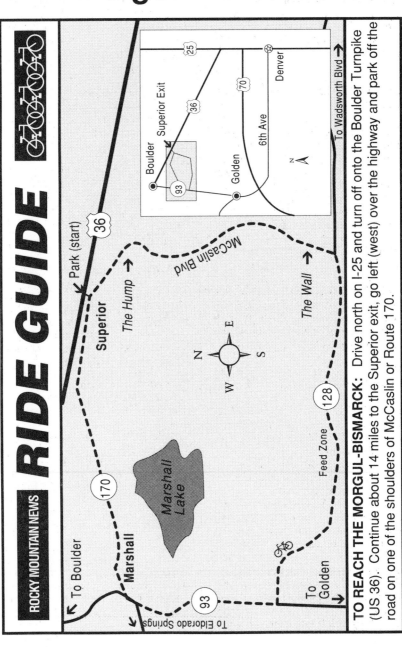

TO REACH THE MORGUL-BISMARCK: Drive north on I-25 and turn off onto the Boulder Turnpike (US 36). Continue about 14 miles to the Superior exit, go left (west) over the highway and park off the road on one of the shoulders of McCaslin or Route 170.

ROCKY MOUNTAIN NEWS *RIDE GUIDE*

BICYCLE: This route was designed for a racing bike, but you can have lots of fun here on your touring or mountain bike. The less knobby the tires, the better.

SURFACE: These county roads are smooth and well maintained. In winter and spring, watch for sand on the shoulders on The Hump, The Wall, Route 128 and the descent down Route 93.

DISTANCE: One lap of this race course is 13 miles.

DIFICULTY: This ride is moderate to difficult with several short, hard climbs. Total climbing over the route is about 1100 vertical feet and includes some steep grades.

RIDE TIME: You will probably spend nearly an hour or more to complete the loop. World class racers average near 30 minutes per lap (about 25 mph) over eight circuits of the course.

THE ROUTE: Head south on McCaslin Blvd. and start climbing The Hump, a brief but attention getting hill. A quick descent for a mile will position you to begin the mile and a half climb to The Wall. Rest on the descent because you'll need all your energy to get over The Wall; it's steep.

As you climb The Wall consider that Russian racer Victor Demidenko was said to have made this climb in his big chainring. Once at the top, take a right at the T onto Route 128 and catch your breath on the half mile coast to the next climb.

This hill is generally referred to as the Feed Zone, the area on a road race course where racers pick up their "musette bags" filled with the appropriate nourishment. Not as steep as where you've been, you will crest the highest point on the route (5995 ft.) and dip down again for another mile.

Another brief, easy climb will put you at the intersection of Route 93. Go right and prepare for a fast three mile descent. Stay to the right and under control; there can be auto traffic on 93, depending on the time of day.

Look for Route 170 (Marshall), slow down, and go right towards Superior. There is an intersection immediately after you make the turn onto 170 where you will take another right and finish the loop back to McCaslin and your car.

If you are training for one of the longer recreational rides this summer, take another lap or two. The Morgul-Bismarck course is an excellent place to condition yourself for riding varied terrain. It does not, however, prepare you for long climbs up mountain passes; we will help you with that in a future *RIDE GUIDE*.

SHIFTING GEARS: Why Morgul-Bismarck? Apparently, the original designers of this route felt compelled to name it after their dog and cat. Don't ask me....

Morrison via Bear Creek

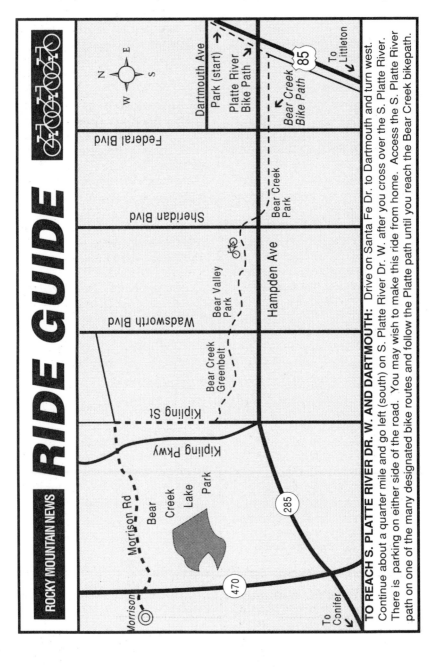

ROCKY MOUNTAIN NEWS

RIDE GUIDE

TO REACH S. PLATTE RIVER DR. W. AND DARTMOUTH: Drive on Santa Fe Dr. to Dartmouth and turn west. Continue about a quarter mile and go left (south) on S. Platte River Dr. W. after you cross over the S. Platte River. There is parking on either side of the road. You may wish to make this ride from home. Access the S. Platte River path on one of the many designated bike routes and follow the Platte path until you reach the Bear Creek bikepath.

Dartmouth Ave
Park (start)
Platte River
Bike Path

Bear Creek Bike Path

85

To
Littleton

Federal Blvd

Bear Creek
Park

Sheridan Blvd

Hampden Ave

Bear Valley
Park

Wadsworth Blvd

Bear Creek
Greenbelt

Kipling St

Kipling Pkwy

Morrison Rd

Bear
Creek
Lake
Park

285

470

To
Conifer

Morrison

ROCKY MOUNTAIN NEWS *RIDE GUIDE*

BICYCLE: This ride is comfortable on either a road or mountain bike.

SURFACE: The entire ride is on well maintained bike path and county roads.

DISTANCE: Round trip to Morrison is about 25 miles.

DIFFICULTY: This ride is easy, but includes one moderately hard climb over the hill to Morrison.

RIDE TIME: Riding time should be between two and three hours.

THE ROUTE: From your parking place on South Platte River Drive West, get on the Platte River bikeway and head south. About three hundred yards after you ride under Hampden Avenue bear right when the path forks and continue west on the Bear Creek bike path.

As you roll west you will cross over the creek a number of times. Notice the beaver gnawed trees along the creek, so close to a residential neighborhood. Follow signs for the Colorado Greenway; if you find you are riding away from the creek, you have made a wrong turn.

Just before Sheridan Boulevard the path dips under Hampden again and dumps you into the parking lot of the Bear Valley Shopping Center. Follow the creek until the path appears once more.

After you pass Sheridan, you'll wind your way through Bear Valley Park, and after Wadsworth, the path twists through the Bear Creek

Greenbelt and ends at Kipling Street. There is a sign "Bike Path Ends" at Kipling. Recently, I spotted a large Osprey in a tree near this location.

Go right on Kipling Street for a half mile and left (west) on Morrison Road. Continue west to Morrison. After you cross Kipling Parkway the road becomes two lanes in both directions and has a large shoulder. Bear Creek Lake Park is on your left as you make the one mile climb over the hill.

In Morrison you can find something to eat and drink. If you are still itching for more riding, take a side trip through Red Rocks Park. The entrance is on the right at the west end of town. Otherwise, return to Denver the way you came.

MAPS: Denver Bicycle Touring Club: Bicycling Denver Route Map; Colorado Division of Parks: Colorado Urban Trails Guide; Denver street guide or metro map.

SHIFTING GEARS: Thorns can be a problem on the bikepaths. You can purchase tire liners and thorn resistant tubes, but they're heavy.

Make sure your tires are always inflated to max (hard), stay off the sides of the paths, carry two extra tubes, and practice changing flats.

If you experience a thorn attack, make sure to carefully check your tire (run your hand all the way around the <u>inside</u> of the tire to locate the perpetrators) when replacing the tube.

Mosquito Pass

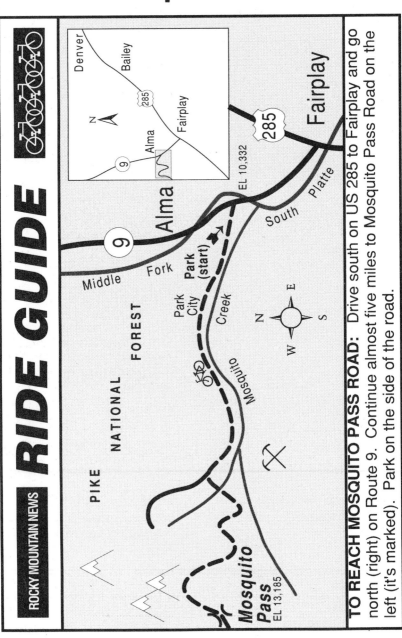

ROCKY MOUNTAIN NEWS *RIDE GUIDE*

Denver
Bailey
285
Fairplay
N
Alma
9

EL 10,332
285
Fairplay

Alma
Platte
South
9
Middle   Fork   Park
Park   (start)
City
Creek
N
E
W   S

Mosquito

PIKE   NATIONAL   FOREST

Mosquito
Pass
EL 13,185

TO REACH MOSQUITO PASS ROAD: Drive south on US 285 to Fairplay and go north (right) on Route 9. Continue almost five miles to Mosquito Pass Road on the left (it's marked). Park on the side of the road.

BICYCLE: Mountain bike.

SURFACE: Smooth gravel road becomes rockier as you ascend, then turns to rough shelf road.

DISTANCE: The round trip is about 20 miles.

DIFFICULTY: This ride is difficult. It's not long in terms of mileage, but it's steep and rocky. The average grade over the ten miles is about six percent, with the final three miles to the top averaging 12 percent over rocky road.

RIDE TIME: Allow at least three and a half hours.

CAUTION: Sunny skies can quickly degenerate at higher elevations, especially above 11,000 feet, and even in mid summer. Essential equipment for this ride is a rain jacket with hood, rain pants and full finger gloves.

If thunderheads in the area produce lightning, it's time to expeditiously make your way quickly to lower and less exposed elevations.

GREAT VIEWS: Panoramic high country vista of the Continental Divide and Colorado's highest four-teeners is ample reward for the stiff pedaling to reach the top.

MAPS: US Forest Service: San Isabel National Forest; USGS 30 x 60 minute: Leadville, Colo.

THE ROUTE: The stage road over Mosquito Pass was born out of the silver and gold rush of the late 19th century. At the time, it was the fastest access from Denver to fortunes in Leadville.

Horse-drawn wagons hauled people and freight over this passage until 1881. There was even an inn perched high on the pass that served as a halfway rest stop on the trip to Leadville. (The Stagecoach Inn still exists in the reconstructed gold camp of South Park City, next to Fairplay.)

Heading west on the Mosquito Pass road, you will pedal through the hamlet of Park City at about two miles. Mosquito Creek is to the left and, indeed, breeds those little pests from which it takes its name.

Denver mountain bike frame builder Wayne Evans joined me on a recent assault to test his superlative Mt. Evans mountain bikes.

The road becomes a little rougher as you climb out of the valley past remnants of the mining era. The gain is moderate but steady.

At about seven miles, you'll emerge above timberline and the road forks. Bend around to the left (it's marked) and take a break at the "old stagecoach" sign.

Look up the basin at Mosquito Peak, Mount Buckskin and Mount Democrat towering to the north.

Shift your tractor into low gear for the steep pitches and switchbacks ahead. A mile and a half farther, the road twists through still more old mining shacks, then becomes rockier as you wind around London Mountain.

On the last mile to the summit, the views intensify, but you will probably be preoccupied with the obstacle course beneath the wheels.

At the pass, look down at Leadville tucked well below Mount Massive and Mount Elbert to the west. If you walk a short way off the pass to the north, a full view of the Collegiate Range unfolds to the south.

Oh-My-God Road

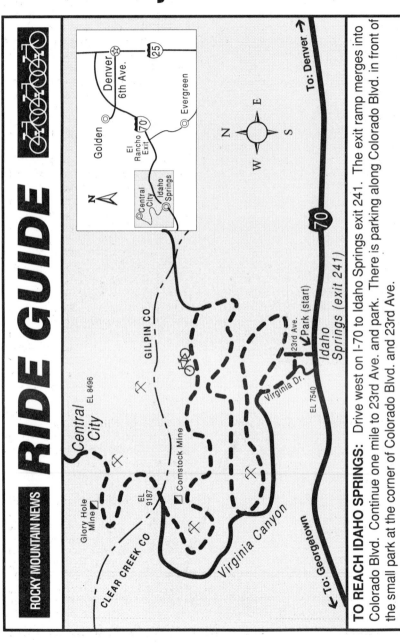

TO REACH IDAHO SPRINGS: Drive west on I-70 to Idaho Springs exit 241. The exit ramp merges into Colorado Blvd. Continue one mile to 23rd Ave. and park. There is parking along Colorado Blvd. in front of the small park at the corner of Colorado Blvd. and 23rd Ave.

ROCKY MOUNTAIN NEWS *RIDE GUIDE*

BICYCLE: Mountain bike with dirt tires.

SURFACE: Virginia Canyon Road from Idaho Springs over the hill to Central City is a well maintained gravel road. The road is plowed in winter and on the Idaho Springs side it stays relatively dry due to the southern exposure. The same is not always true on the Central City side. Watch for icy sections.

DISTANCE: Round trip, Idaho Springs to Central City and back is approximately 18 miles.

DIFFICULTY: This route is moderate to difficult with several steep climbs. From Idaho Springs to the top there is a steady gain of 1650 vertical feet. Down to Central City, there is one shorter but steeper hill.

RIDE TIME: The round trip usually takes two and a half or more hours, depending on stops.

THE ROUTE: The Oh-My-God Road (Virginia Canyon Road) was apparently so named when one of our Presidents blurted out the moniker during a trip over to Central City. No — he was not riding a bicycle.

Cross the bridge heading north on 23rd Avenue and take a left on Virginia St. Continue four-tenths of a mile to Virginia Canyon Rd. and go right. These streets are paved. The canyon road will climb steeply for a half mile and just as the pavement ends take a hard right on County Road 279.

The road maintains a constant five plus percent grade to the top. As you switch back, there is a great view of the Squaw Pass Road and the ski area across Clear Creek Canyon to the south. After about two more miles, go hard right once again at the intersection. Check out the old mines as you finish the last steady pedalling to the top.

I save this ride for late autumn, winter, and early spring. It's rideable all winter, even on hard packed snow, and provides an excellent workout. The temperature can be extremely cold on top, especially with the wind blowing, so take your coldest weather gear in winter.

The descent to Central City is gradual at first, but the last mile is steep and fast. This part of the ride has a northern exposure, so watch for sections of ice in the winter and wet muddy spots in the spring.

You'll pass some old mines including the famous Glory Hole Mine.

In Central City there are several restaurants where you can eat breakfast or lunch or just enjoy a cup of hot tea, before returning the way you came.

MAPS: U.S.G.S.: 7.5 minute Idaho Springs and Central City; 30 X 60 minute Denver West. U.S. Forest Service: Arapaho National Forest.

Peru Creek

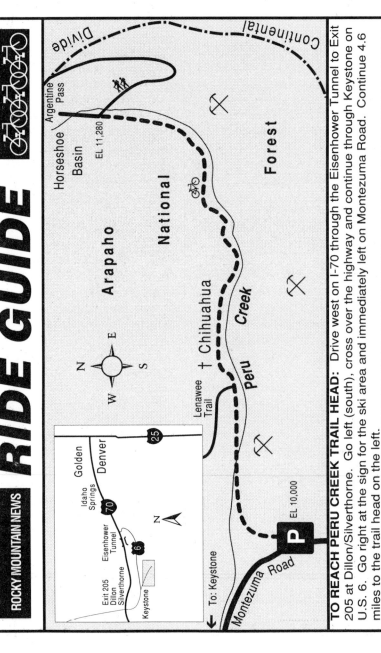

ROCKY MOUNTAIN NEWS

RIDE GUIDE

TO REACH PERU CREEK TRAIL HEAD: Drive west on I-70 through the Eisenhower Tunnel to Exit 205 at Dillon/Silverthorne. Go left (south), cross over the highway and continue through Keystone on U.S. 6. Go right at the sign for the ski area and immediately left on Montezuma Road. Continue 4.6 miles to the trail head on the left.

BICYCLE: Mountain bike.

SURFACE: Peru Creek Road has a relatively smooth dirt surface. There are some rocky sections, however, especially at the high point of the ride.

DISTANCE: The round trip is about ten miles.

DIFFICULTY: The route is easy to moderate because of several short steep climbs, and a very rocky section near the top. All of the riding is above 10,000 feet.

RIDE TIME: Allow at least two hours.

MAPS: The Mountain Bike Guide to Summit County; USGS 7.5 minute: Montezuma.

THE ROUTE: Summit County has become well known for the network of wonderful paved bike paths linking its resort towns. However, some of the best mountain bike riding is on the many spectacular backcountry trails.

If you're ready to get off the beaten path, there are a number of options to reach the high country on exciting mountain bike routes.

Peru Creek Road ambles gradually through the once flourishing mining camps of the area and halts in precipitous Horseshoe Basin. High above, the Continental Divide wraps around the basin from north to south.

On a spring ride, local mountain bike trail expert Laura Rossetter identified the numerous points of interest.

From the trail head parking lot, start pedalling north on Peru Creek Road. At about one mile, you will span Peru Creek and ride parallel to the creek on your right.

Look for the Lenawee Trail on the left another half mile up the road. It winds over Lenawee Mountain to Arapahoe Basin.

At two miles Warden Gulch is on the right, but you must ford the creek to get to it.

Continue east (straight) for not quite half a mile to the former mining settlement of Chihuahua. The old graveyard there has recently been marked with a single headstone. In its heyday the mine apparently was serviced by cable car.

At approximately two and a half miles you will make a short, steep climb and level out with the creek bubbling just to your right; look for several beaver ponds.

After another short ascent, a meadow opens ahead as you pedal toward timberline.

Up and to your right, the old Pennsylvania Mine site will come into view. This mine and others in the valley primarily extracted silver from the hills.

Pass through a gate at about four miles. The road begins to get rocky as it bends back to the north. Don't let this stop you; the Argentine Pass trail head is near.

At the trail head take a break and check out the scenery. Grays Peak and Mt. Edwards are to the north and Argentine Peak is to the east.

The Argentine Pass trail traverses the mountain and disappears over the divide to the northeast. There is also a trail that climbs through Horseshoe Basin and up over Grays Peak (14,270 feet); so if you're still feeling spry...

Your return trip can be a fast descent. Be careful to stay in control on the rocky sections.

Rollins Pass

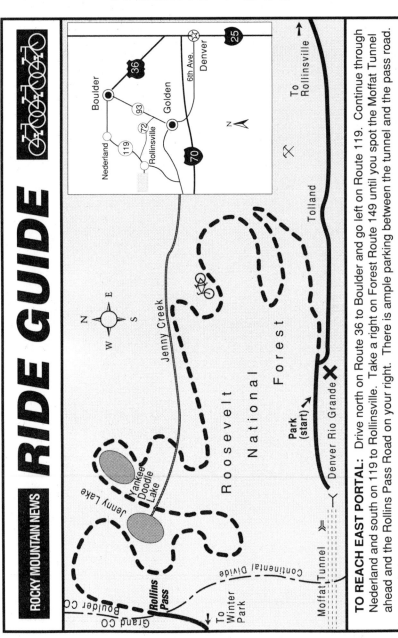

TO REACH EAST PORTAL: Drive north on Route 36 to Boulder and go left on Route 119. Continue through Nederland and south on 119 to Rollinsville. Take a right on Forest Route 149 until you spot the Moffat Tunnel ahead and the Rollins Pass Road on your right. There is ample parking between the tunnel and the pass road.

ROCKY MOUNTAIN NEWS *RIDE GUIDE*

BICYCLE: Mountain bike.

SURFACE: This old railroad bed was once the train passage over the Continental Divide. The rails are now gone, the surface is dirt and it's moderately rocky in sections. Reopened in recent years to four-wheel drive vehicles, you may encounter auto traffic (much less on weekdays and after Labor Day), but the old road is wide enough.

DISTANCE: Round trip, to the top of the pass, and back down is about 29 miles.

DIFFICULTY: The grade is not intense, an average of just over three percent for the 14.5 miles to the top. Because of the distance, and the tolerantly rocky surface, I rate the route as moderate to difficult.

RIDE TIME: Allow three to four hours to complete the ride.

THE ROUTE: Before the construction of the Moffat Tunnel on the Denver and Rio Grande Western Railroad line, train access to the high country over the Continental Divide meant a white knuckle climb over Rollins Pass and a wide-eyed descent to Winter Park. These days, riders can pale their knuckles on their mountain bike with a fun and invigorating workout on the old railroad bed.

Although you will reach an altitude of 11,671 feet at the top, the approximate 2,500-foot gain does not represent steep riding. For trains to have climbed this route, the grade could not be too severe.

Starting up the road, you will be heading back to the east for the initial two and a half miles. Then,

the path hairpins and steers you back to the west.

At about six miles, the Jenny Creek Trail is on the right. This hiking trail parallels the road up to Yankee Doodle Lake and provides access to other good cross country ski trails in winter.

Four more miles and you will reach Yankee Doodle Lake. This is an appropriate place to take a break before the final four and a half miles to the pass.

On the last leg to the summit you will ride through the Needle, a tunnel in the rock that was renovated several years ago. You will also encounter several wooden tressels that cling to the mountain just this side of the divide. The Forest Service has diverted traffic around the tressels for obvious safety reasons, so take heed.

The views from the top, and during the ascent, are spectacular. Look to the north for a sensational glimpse into the Indian Peaks Wilderness Area and Rocky Mountain National Park. To the west are the Vasquez and Williams Fork mountains.

The descent is fast and great fun. Some of the rockier sections will shake you up a bit and give your upper body a little workout from holding on and braking. Be careful to stay under control, and be looking for an occasional auto.

Take plenty of water (at least two bottles) and some food. The weather may change, so be prepared with warm clothes: rain gear and gloves, especially in the fall.

MAPS: Trails Illustrated: Rollins Pass; U.S. Forest: Roosevelt National Forest, Arapaho National Forest.

Sedalia to Perry Park

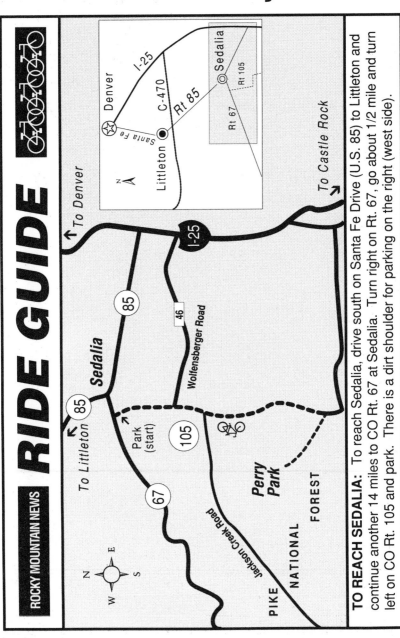

TO REACH SEDALIA: To reach Sedalia, drive south on Santa Fe Drive (U.S. 85) to Littleton and continue another 14 miles to CO Rt. 67 at Sedalia. Turn right on Rt. 67, go about 1/2 mile and turn left on CO Rt. 105 and park. There is a dirt shoulder for parking on the right (west side).

ROCKY MOUNTAIN NEWS *RIDE GUIDE*

BICYCLE: Road bike, although mountain bikes will do. The less knobby the tires, the better.

SURFACE: The paved surface of Colo. 105 is smooth and very well maintained. The shoulders are good, but sometimes narrow. Watch for sand in the Spring.

DISTANCE: Round trip will be about 30 miles.

DIFFICULTY: The route is easy to moderate, but rolling, and gains only a few hundred vertical feet in the 14 miles out to Perry Park.

RIDE TIME: Should take between two and four hours.

GREAT VIEWS: The view of the Front Range is magnificent on a clear day. Due west is Long Scraggy Peak, to the southwest you'll see the Rampart Range and the Taryall Mountains and, of course, to the south is Pikes Peak. Colo. 105 cuts through some lovely rural, Front Range farm country.

THE ROUTE: If you've had it with the stop signs and red lights around town, you need only drive a short distance from Denver to enjoy a scenic road ride along the Front Range. The Sedalia to Perry Park ride offers non-stop pedaling while accommodating a wide range of fitness levels.

As with many state roads, the paved shoulder portion of 105 is narrow in places. Plan to maintain single file where necessary. Auto traffic is at a minimum early on Saturday and Sunday mornings.

Four and a half miles down 105, Wolfensberger Road (County 46) intersects to the left. Another two miles and Jackson Creek Road will be to the right; there's some great mountain bike riding up that one. At about 14 miles, the road to Perry Park is on the right and marked. After a short climb, you'll descend into this lovely residential area. If you bear right at the fork at the bottom of the hill, and go past the golf course, you can climb some moderate hills for a good view of the area. Perry Park offers opportunities for leisurely exploring.

MAPS: Colorado road map or road atlas. U.S. Forest Service: Pike National Forest.

KEEP IN MIND: There is no food, water, or public bathrooms on this route. You should take some food and at least two waterbottles. There are several convenience/grocery stores in Sedalia where you can stock up.

SHIFTING GEARS: The 1988 Colorado House Bill No. 1246 concerning bicycle traffic laws states "Every person riding a bicycle shall have all of the rights and duties applicable to the driver of any other vehicle...". For all the new bicycle laws and for city and state bicycle maps, contact the Colorado Department of Highways.

Shrine Pass

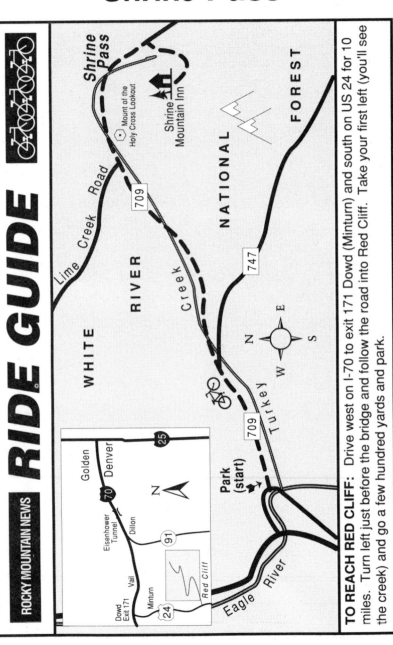

TO REACH RED CLIFF: Drive west on I-70 to exit 171 Dowd (Minturn) and south on US 24 for 10 miles. Turn left just before the bridge and follow the road into Red Cliff. Take your first left (you'll see the creek) and go a few hundred yards and park.

ROCKY MOUNTAIN NEWS *RIDE GUIDE*

BICYCLE: Mountain bike.

SURFACE: Smooth gravel Forest Route, with a few minimally rocky sections.

DISTANCE: The ride to the inn and back is about 19 miles. (If you skip the inn and ride to Shrine Pass and return, then the mileage is about one mile less.)

DIFFICULTY: This ride is moderate to difficult. The route gradually gains over 2400 vertical feet in the nine and a half miles to the top.

RIDE TIME: Allow at least three hours; schedule additional time for lunch.

MAPS: US Forest Service: White River National Forest.

SPECIAL FEATURE: In recommending backcountry roads for good mountain bike rides, I usually suggest the one less traveled by. These roads (or trails) don't typically lead to a restaurant for lunch.

But in the case of the Shrine Mountain Inn, I feel the deviation is an enhancement to the ride.

The inn sits just above Shrine Pass at an elevation of 11,209 feet. Privately owned, it is part of a hut system contiguous to the Tenth Mountain Trail that links Vail to Aspen.

These huts are used primarily for cross country skiing, but some have been made available to hikers and mountain bikers in the summer.

The Shrine Mountain Inn serves a reasonably priced lunch (11am to 2pm except Monday), on the deck of Chuck's Cabin, July 4th weekend through Labor Day weekend – best

to check with the Inn for changes. This is a wonderful way to take a break from the pedaling, enjoy the views and support a very worthwhile backcountry project.

THE ROUTE: The Shrine Pass Road (Forest Route 709) was the old route to Glenwood Springs before US 6 was constructed through the Gore Valley. In recent years, it probably is best known as a magnificent cross country ski trail.

The road climbs from Red Cliff beside Turkey Creek maintaining about a five percent grade for the trip to the top. Aerobics expert Peggy Lilienthal set the pace on a recent mid summer luncheon run.

At just over two miles, Forest Route 747 is on the right; it climbs along Wearyman Creek, over Ptarmigan Pass and down to Camp Hale via Resolution Creek.

The valley begins to open another half mile further, but the road remains sheltered in a beautiful pine forest.

At four miles, you'll break out of the pines into a meadow where old cabins pose. There's a sign at the edge of the meadow with the word "toilet" and an arrow pointing into the woods.

There's a short steep climb to the six mile mark. Look back for a good view of the Sawatch Range.

The road forks one half mile further; follow the switchback around to the left.

At seven and a half miles the observation area for the Mount of the Holy Cross is on the right and worth checking out. And at nine miles, the entrance to the inn is on the right; you can't miss the red gate. Chuck's Cabin is not quite a half mile up the drive.

Take the Family to Chatfield

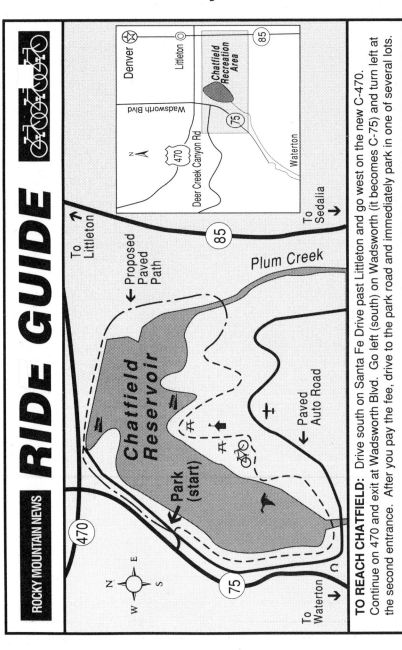

ROCKY MOUNTAIN NEWS — *RIDE GUIDE*

TO REACH CHATFIELD: Drive south on Santa Fe Drive past Littleton and go west on the new C-470. Continue on 470 and exit at Wadsworth Blvd. Go left (south) on Wadsworth (it becomes C-75) and turn left at the second entrance. After you pay the fee, drive to the park road and immediately park in one of several lots.

ROCKY MOUNTAIN NEWS **RIDE GUIDE**

BICYCLE: Almost any style of bicycle is appropriate for this recreation area.

SURFACE: Almost all the riding is entirely on bike paths. The paths are generally in good condition. However, certain sections that lie close to the reservoir may sit under water during the winter and spring and consequently they can be a little rough. Be prepared to circumvent wet spots on the bike paths in the early spring.

DISTANCE: The round trip to Plum Creek and back to your car is about 12 miles.

DIFFICULTY: Easy riding. Chatfield is perfect for the entire family.

RIDE TIME: There are so many opportunities to observe and participate in activities that the time spent at Chatfield will depend on you. Plan on two hours minimum.

WILDLIFE: Over 180 species of birds have been spotted, with the most notable being the Great Blue Heron. Beaver, muskrats, deer, coyotes, rabbits and foxes are also residents of the area.

THE ROUTE: Chatfield State Recreation Area is a wonderful place for the whole family to enjoy a day of cycling and other activities. It is leased and administrated by the Colorado Division of Parks and Outdoor Recreation and consequently a fee of $3.00 per car is charged to enter and park. This helps to fund operations and is worth every penny. Ask for a map when you pay the fee at the entrance station.

From your parking place you will find the bike path between the park road and the lake. Notice the swim beach just off the parking lot; you may want to plan a swim after you finish the ride.

The bike path takes you south for nearly two miles and then bends to the east and crosses the South Platte River. Just before the river there is an extension of the path that goes south, but only for a short distance before running out of hard surface.

Once you cross the Platte, you will pedal to the north for a mile where there is an overlook for the Heron Rookery. Don't fail to stop and check out these amazing birds nesting in the tops of trees in the lake.

Nearby is a model airplane airport, but you will need to access it from the park road. This is easy from the overlook; ride up to the parking lot, go left on the park road and take your first right. There will probably be planes buzzing overhead; this is fun for everyone.

Retrace your route back to the bike path and continue north to Lakeview, Marina Point and The Fishing Pier. Take your pole.

From here the path winds southeast through the campgrounds and disappears before you reach Plum Creek. There is a long term plan to complete the path as an entire circuit of the lake. Look for progress.

The Training Race

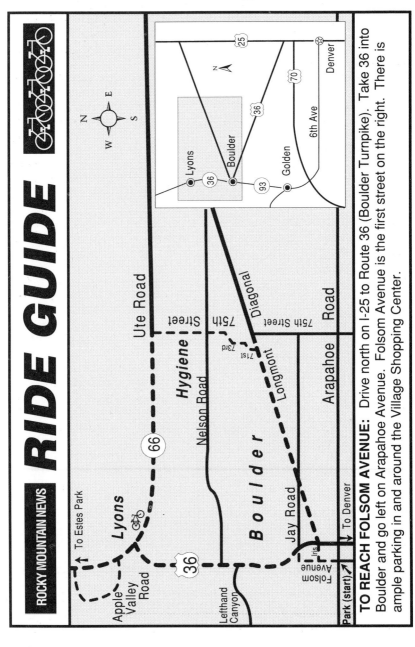

TO REACH FOLSOM AVENUE: Drive north on I-25 to Route 36 (Boulder Turnpike). Take 36 into Boulder and go left on Arapahoe Avenue. Folsom Avenue is the first street on the right. There is ample parking in and around the Village Shopping Center.

ROCKY MOUNTAIN NEWS *RIDE GUIDE*

BICYCLE: This ride is most comfortable on a road bike, but can be ridden on a mountain bike as well.

SURFACE: The road surface for the entire loop is excellent. The shoulders (or bike lane in some places) are wide. Watch for sand in the spring.

DISTANCE: The loop is about 42 miles.

DIFFICULTY: The pedaling is easy on mildly rolling terrain. Because of the distance, the ride is easy to moderate.

RIDE TIME: Allow three hours to complete the loop.

THE ROUTE: This ride follows much of the route used for the sometimes infamous and now defunct Boulder Training Race. As many as 100 racers of all calibers jammed the roadways in pursuit of better skills every Tuesday and Thursday evening, much to the consternation of auto traffic and the local police.

U.S. 36 from Lyons to Boulder was also the final section of the Coors Classic's Boulder Mountain Road Race, possibly remembered most for the police road block that interrupted the finish in 1985.

This route remains well cycled today. This is no surprise considering the wide, smooth shoulders and magnificent scenery. On a recent trip, color commentary was provided by former Coors Classic staffer and Boulder bon vivant Dan Craig.

From your parking spot, head north on Folsom; at almost two miles it turns into 26th Street. Go another half mile and right on Jay, then immediately left on Route 36.

At 15 miles, bear to the left on U.S. 36 at the stop light. Go through Lyons and ride another mile and a half, then follow 36 to the right . You're still heading north.

Look for Old Apple Valley Road on your left; it's another two tenths of a mile. This is a country road with a gentle stream running alongside.

In two and a half miles you will meet U.S. 36 again, where you go right (south).

Continue back through Lyons, the way you came, except don't go right at the stop light on the east side of town. Instead, continue east on U.S. 66 (Ute Road).

Pedal four miles and take a right on 75th Street (there's a sign for Hygiene). Look to your right for a great view of Longs Peak.

Hygiene's a mile down the road and is a good place for food and drink, if you're in need.

Another mile further, look for a llama farm on the right. You will also have a wonderful view of the Front Range to the south.

The intersection of Nelson Road is just ahead. Here, a large group on the Boulder Training Race neglected to stop at the stop sign, and all were greeted by the police and issued the appropriate paperwork.

Seventy-fifth Street jogs right into 73rd Street which jogs right into 71st Street and joins the Diagonal Highway. Go right on the Diagonal for about four miles and exit to the right (west) at the intersection with the Foothills Parkway.

Continue across 28th Street (Route 36) on Iris Avenue to Folsom and turn left. Take Folsom back to your auto.

Tour de South Suburbia

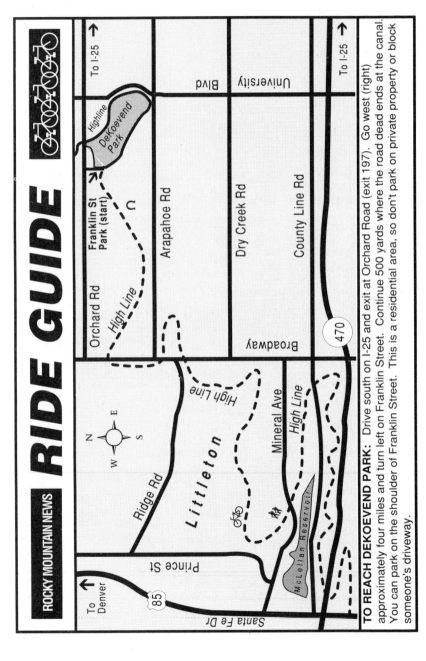

RIDE GUIDE

ROCKY MOUNTAIN NEWS

TO REACH DEKOEVEND PARK: Drive south on I-25 and exit at Orchard Road (exit 197). Go west (right) approximately four miles and turn left on Franklin Street. Continue 500 yards where the road dead ends at the canal. You can park on the shoulder of Franklin Street. This is a residential area, so don't park on private property or block someone's driveway.

ROCKY MOUNTAIN NEWS **RIDE GUIDE**

BICYCLE: This route requires a mountain bike. In summer, when the surface is hard and dry, a road bike would work, but it will not be as comfortable as a fatter tire style bicycle.

SURFACE: This part of the High Line Canal trail has the original dirt surface. It is generally smooth and well maintained. However, be forewarned that in the early spring there may be some muddy sections. Also, many equestrians use the trail, so be on the lookout for those incommodious obstacles that horses leave behind.

DISTANCE: The round trip from DeKoevend Park to Santa Fe Drive and back is about 22 miles.

DIFFICULTY: The actual pedaling is easy, but because of the distance, I would rate this ride as easy to moderate. Remember that riding a bicycle on dirt is considerably more strenuous than riding on pavement.

RIDE TIME: The round trip should take three hours or more to complete.

THE ROUTE: The southern most portion of the High Line Canal zig-zags through ever changing suburbia on its way to the foothills. The route begins within the older residential neighborhoods of this area, weaves a path through brand new commercial and residential developments, and finally emerges in the yet undisturbed land south of County Line Road. The diversification of scenery makes the riding more interesting and fun.

Start pedaling to the west (right) on the High Line Canal Trail. You will soon cross Clarkson Street on the way to the first of three traverses of South Broadway. "As the crow flies", this route would be less than half the distance of the meandering trail.

You will likely encounter equestrians on the trail, especially on the weekends. Because mountain bikes are "new kids on the block", many horses are not familiar with them. Please use every courtesy when passing horses; you should always yield to them. When approaching from behind, make sure that equestrians are aware of you and let them signal you by before you make an attempt to pass. Most mountain biking is done on trails that are shared by several user types; cyclists can avoid a bad name through simple courtesy.

After crossing Broadway for the third time, look for the occasional glimpses of the Front Range. The view becomes increasingly spectacular as you continue south across Mineral Avenue towards McLellan Reservoir.

After spanning County Line Road, and at about the seven-mile mark, turn right (west) on a paved section for two miles. Immediately after the tunnel under 470, go left onto the dirt again for the last two miles. The route ends at Santa Fe Drive just east of Chatfield Reservoir.

Tour de Two Forks

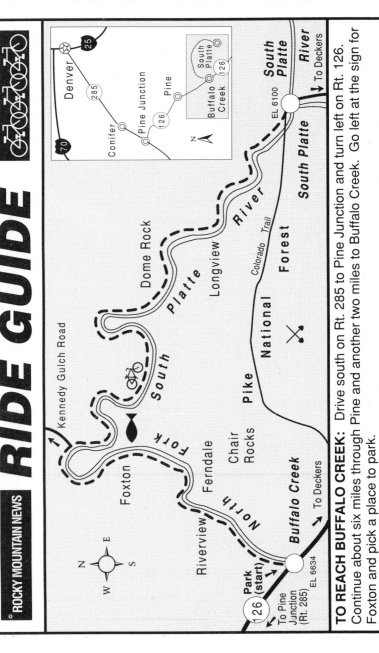

TO REACH BUFFALO CREEK: Drive south on Rt. 285 to Pine Junction and turn left on Rt. 126. Continue about six miles through Pine and another two miles to Buffalo Creek. Go left at the sign for Foxton and pick a place to park.

ROCKY MOUNTAIN NEWS **RIDE GUIDE**

BICYCLE: This is a mountain bike ride.

SURFACE: CountyRoad 96 is a dirt road that follows the North Fork of the South Platte River. It is relatively smooth, as dirt roads go, but you are likely to shake over some washboard sections in the spring. On weekends in the warmer months, when the anglers, kayakers and picnickers drive in to do their thing, you may eat some dust off the dry road.

DISTANCE: The round trip from Buffalo Creek to South Platte and back is approximately 20 miles.

DIFFICULTY: The actual pedaling is easy; the grade is about one percent coming back upstream from South Platte. The total distance of 20 miles makes the ride a little harder. Remember that 20 miles on a dirt road on your mountain bike is more strenuous than on pavement.

RIDE TIME: Plan on spending two to three hours or more.

THE ROUTE: This family ride along the North Fork of the South Platte cuts through some of the rugged, rocky terrain of the northern-most boundary of the Pike National Forest. The route follows the final ten miles of river before its confluence with the South Platte River at the proposed and controversial Two Forks Dam site.

During the warmer months, this section of river attracts a wide variety of recreational enthusiasts. There is usually ample diversion from the road in the form of scenery, wildlife and other recreational activities.

Head downstream (east) from Buffalo Creek and the river will be on your right. Look up to see a number of massive rock outcroppings; Cathedral Spires is to the left and Chair Rocks to the right.

You'll ride through some tiny residential communities, Riverview, Ferndale and Foxton. Twisting and turning your way within the canyon, Kennedy Gulch Road (maybe better known as Foxton Road) joins 96 on the left at about five miles.

The fishing in this section of river is supposed to be quite good, and the many anglers dotting the banks in summer must be testimony to the fact. They seem to range from the serious types with waders to the fair-weather, lounge chair sportsmen with line tied around big toe.

Continuing east to the one-time hamlet of South Platte (currently, I don't believe anyone actually lives there), the communities of Dome Rock and Longview are along the road. In this area, I have seen a number of kayakers floating some fairly rapid sections of the river

In South Platte, check out the old and dilapidated hotel. Just past the hotel and before the bridge, bear to the right and ride down to the bank for a close view of the confluence of these two great rivers.

The ride back will be a little harder than the trip out, but don't be concerned. Remember to take a wind breaker in case the weather changes, and take plenty of water because you won't find any along the route. There is, however, a gas station with some basic groceries in Buffalo Creek.

Trail to Meadows Campground

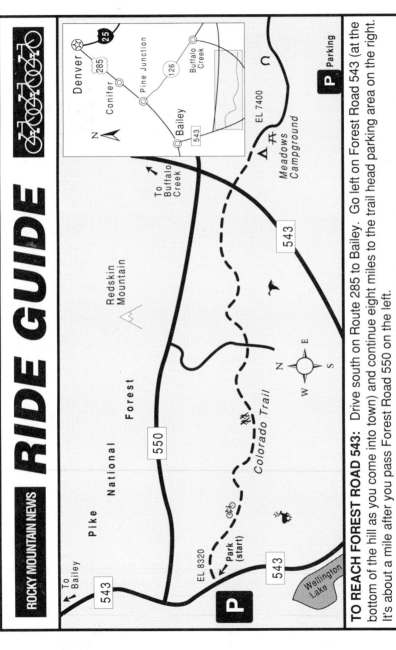

RIDE GUIDE

ROCKY MOUNTAIN NEWS

TO REACH FOREST ROAD 543: Drive south on Route 285 to Bailey. Go left on Forest Road 543 (at the bottom of the hill as you come into town) and continue eight miles to the trail head parking area on the right. It's about a mile after you pass Forest Road 550 on the left.

ROCKY MOUNTAIN NEWS **RIDE GUIDE**

BICYCLE: A mountain bike with good off-road tires.

SURFACE: This single track trail is smooth and very rideable. There are some small stream crossings.

DISTANCE: The round trip is about eight miles.

DIFFICULTY: The ride is moderately difficult. There is an elevation loss of nearly 1,000 vertical feet going out, so save a little energy for the trip back. Also, there is a relatively steep section of about a half mile.

RIDE TIME: Plan on a minimum of two and a half hours.

THE ROUTE: This short section of the Colorado Trail is best suited for the mountain biker who has some off-road experience, especially on single tracks. While not difficult and not a long ride, basic mountain bike handling skills should be in place before one sets out on this route.

The Colorado Trail was designed for family use, and consequently it flows gently along, unless a pass or saddle needs to be spanned. This section is consistent with the design, except for one steep hill, and makes for some of the best off-road riding through the rugged Pike National Forest.

From the trail head parking area, cross Forest Road 543, find the trail head and pedal up the embankment to the east. After the short climb, the trail dips down through a stream and starts up again for about a quarter of a mile.

Once you have leveled out, you will begin twisting and turning through stands of pine and aspen trees on a thrilling but tame descent. Be careful not to get out of control; the trail is lined closely with trees in many places.

At slightly over two miles, the trail intersects a forest road. You may hear gunshots; apparently, there is a gun club at the end of this road to the right.

Continue across the road and pick up the trail (look for the markers). Next, only a few hundred yards later, you will pass several large rock outcroppings. Make sure to stop, either now or on the return, and take in the great view to the southwest.

For the next mile the riding is downhill with the last half steep and tricky. I have experienced some rocks and branches on this descent in the spring, and there is loose dirt come summertime.

At the bottom of this steep hill the trail veers sharply right and dips down into a gully, then back to the left and up over an embankment onto Forest Road 543. Watch for the occasional auto.

Cross 543 and continue briefly along the South Fork of Buffalo Creek. The trail bends off to the right and up a small hill to a gate through a barbed wire fence. Make certain to secure the latch.

The last few hundred yards finishes climbing the hill, and deposits you in Meadows Campground.

For ice cold spring water (only during the warmer months), ride up the campground road to the right for an eighth of a mile; the pump is on the right.

MAPS: Colorado Trail Map

Upper Bear Creek Road

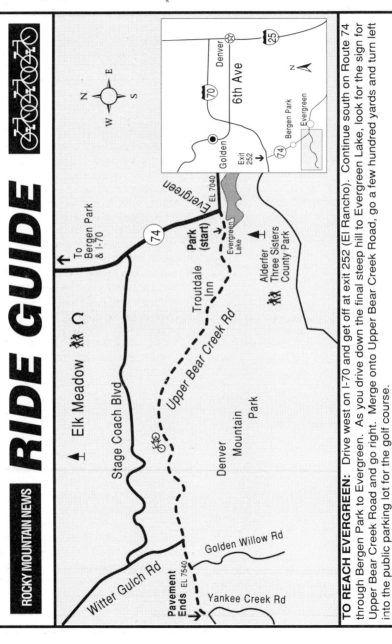

RIDE GUIDE

ROCKY MOUNTAIN NEWS

Elk Meadow

To Bergen Park & I-70

74

Stage Coach Blvd

Troutdale Inn

Park (start)

Upper Bear Creek Rd

Denver Mountain Park

Evergreen

EL 7040

Evergreen Lake

Alderfer Three Sisters County Park

Golden Willow Rd

Witter Gulch Rd

Pavement Ends EL 7540

Yankee Creek Rd

Denver

25

70

6th Ave

Golden

Exit 252

74

Bergen Park

Evergreen

TO REACH EVERGREEN: Drive west on I-70 and get off at exit 252 (El Rancho). Continue south on Route 74 through Bergen Park to Evergreen. As you drive down the final steep hill to Evergreen Lake, look for the sign for Upper Bear Creek Road and go right. Merge onto Upper Bear Creek Road, go a few hundred yards and turn left into the public parking lot for the golf course.

ROCKY MOUNTAIN NEWS **RIDE GUIDE**

BICYCLE: Either road or mountain bikes will be comfortable on this route.

SURFACE: Well maintained county road. The shoulders are narrow in places and there will be sand on the shoulders in the spring.

DISTANCE: The round trip is about 12 miles.

DIFFICULTY: The route is relatively easy, gently gaining altitude going out, but only 500 vertical feet.

RIDE TIME: Plan on about two hours for the round trip.

THE ROUTE: Upper Bear Creek Road boasts many of the most opulent homes in foothills suburbia. Numerous notable types are said to make their summer residences along this tranquil creek. There are also some magnificent old structures that add to the visual pleasure of this leisurely bike ride.

Heading west on Upper Bear Creek, the Evergreen Golf Course is on the left. After a half-mile you will pass the International Bell Museum on the right. This museum claims to have the largest collection of bells in the world. It is only open in the warmer months, however.

Continuing west, make sure to stay far right when rounding the tight bends in the road. The shoulders are narrow so you will want to ride single file. Generally, there is not a great deal of auto traffic, although, in summer, this road is the access to trails in the Mount Evans Wilderness Area.

At one mile, the old Troutdale Inn is on the right. This spectacular structure once operated as a 152-room hotel. Apparently, it became run-down and finally closed in 1963. Many famous guests, including several presidents, are said to have stayed there during its heyday. There is a possibility the property will be renovated and reopened in the future.

For the next few miles, there are many beautiful houses. Then the valley opens a bit to reveal other houses built high along the ridge to the north. You will pass Witter Gulch Road at about four miles and Golden Willow Road on the left at four and a half miles. Look up Golden Willow to glimpse the foundation of a house that evidently burned fairly recently.

Finally, at six miles, the road forks. The route to the right leads to the Evans Ranch, and the road to the left climbs more drastically through private land. In both directions the surface immediately becomes dirt, so you may want to make this the turnaround. However, if you're on your mountain bike and feel like more pedaling, do some exploring in either direction.

SHIFTING GEARS: Dogs can sometimes be a hindrance to cyclists by either running in front of your bike or by chasing you. Jefferson County Animal Control offered several recommendations.

Always be cautious when approaching dogs. Steer clear, or if warranted, dismount and walk by, keeping your bike between you and the beast. Use firm commands (don't scream) like "Stay" or "Go home". More times than not, this is effective.

Waterton Canyon

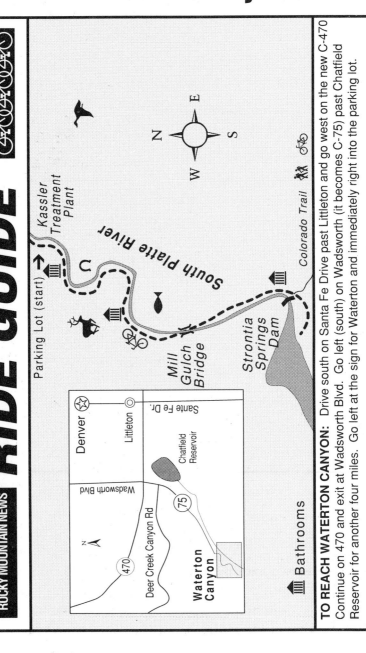

ROCKY MOUNTAIN NEWS *RIDE GUIDE*

Parking Lot (start)

Kassler Treatment Plant

South Platte River

Mill Gulch Bridge

Strontia Springs Dam

Colorado Trail

Bathrooms

Denver

Littleton

Sante Fe Dr.

Wadsworth Blvd

Deer Creek Canyon Rd

Chatfield Reservoir

75

470

Waterton Canyon

TO REACH WATERTON CANYON: Drive south on Santa Fe Drive past Littleton and go west on the new C-470. Continue on 470 and exit at Wadsworth Blvd. Go left (south) on Wadsworth (it becomes C-75) past Chatfield Reservoir for another four miles. Go left at the sign for Waterton and immediately right into the parking lot.

ROCKY MOUNTAIN NEWS **RIDE GUIDE**

BICYCLE: A mountain bike or fatter tire style bike is recommended. However, I have seen many touring bikes in Waterton Canyon, but would advise against using your skinny wheel racing bike.

SURFACE: This old railroad bed has been paved, but it's rough and more like an unpaved road in many places. In the winter the road is plowed and passable, but you may experience snowy or icy spots.

DISTANCE: To the dam and back is 12 miles.

DIFFICULTY: This is an easy ride for the entire family. Because the road follows the South Platte River, upstream going out, and because the road was once the bed for the narrow gauge Denver, South Park and Pacific Railroad, the grade is very gentle. I've seen families with tots to grandparents enjoying themselves.

RIDE TIME: Allow two hours or more for a leisurely round trip.

WILDLIFE: Waterton Canyon is the home for one of the few remaining low altitude herds of bighorn sheep, and it is likely that you may spot one, usually grazing not too far off the road. You may also see a Great Blue Heron fishing in the river or a hawk or eagle soaring overhead.

The canyon supports bobcats, mountain lions, coyotes, foxes, wild turkeys and many other bird species.

THE ROUTE: From the parking lot near the Kassler Water Treatment Plant, push your bike through the opening in the fence, and follow the road, heading upstream. The route and the river twist and turn through the precipitous rock walls of the canyon, and there are numerous opportunities to take a break and enjoy the views.

Absolutely no autos or dogs are allowed, so don't worry about looking over your shoulder, except for the caretaker driving home.

The South Platte River offers choice brown and rainbow trout fishing, and you will see anglers along the entire ride. Incidentally, many of those fishermen have turned cyclist in order to easily reach the great fishing.

The turn-around at Strontia Springs Dam is six miles upstream. You can watch the water pounding into the river from the spillway; in summer the breeze off the dam is air conditioned.

If you continue up the road from the dam, you can access the 470 mile long Colorado Trail, but this is no longer a family ride, unless your name is Carpenter or Phinney. The Colorado Trail will be featured in future editions of the Ride Guide.

On the return trip, look for the start of the High Line Canal on the south side of the river, about two miles from the parking lot.

Waterton Canyon is open year round and is a unique example of an extraordinary natural environment in such close proximity to a major metropolitan area.

MAPS: The U.S. Forest Service and The Division of Wildlife produce a map of Waterton Canyon.

Wellington Lake Loop

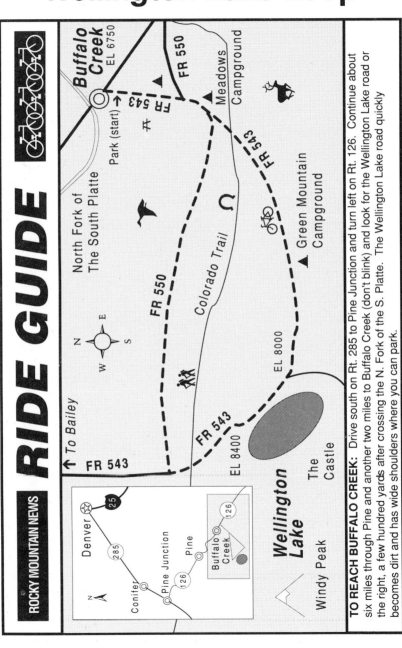

ROCKY MOUNTAIN NEWS

RIDE GUIDE

Buffalo Creek EL 6750

FR 550

FR 543

Meadows Campground

Park (start)

North Fork of The South Platte

FR 550

Colorado Trail

FR 543

Green Mountain Campground

EL 8000

← To Bailey

← FR 543

FR 543

EL 8400

Wellington Lake

The Castle

Windy Peak

Denver

25

285

Conifer

Pine Junction

Pine

126

126

Buffalo Creek

TO REACH BUFFALO CREEK: Drive south on Rt. 285 to Pine Junction and turn left on Rt. 126. Continue about six miles through Pine and another two miles to Buffalo Creek (don't blink) and look for the Wellington Lake road or the right, a few hundred yards after crossing the N. Fork of the S. Platte. The Wellington Lake road quickly becomes dirt and has wide shoulders where you can park.

ROCKY MOUNTAIN NEWS *RIDE GUIDE*

BICYCLE: This is a mountain bike ride.

SURFACE: Well maintained dirt road. You may experience some washboards and/or snowy sections in winter.

DISTANCE: The loop is about 23 miles; if you choose to return from the lake the way you came, then it's about 18 miles.

DIFFICULTY: Moderate, with two short, relatively hard climbs.

RIDE TIME: Allow between two and four hours.

WILDLIFE: In this part of the Pike Forest, I have spotted quail, wild turkeys, eagles, hawks, coyotes and deer.

ELEVATIONS: The route starts at 6800 feet and reaches a high of 8400 feet.

THE ROUTE: The Pike Forest, an hour's auto ride southwest of Denver, offers several wonderful bike rides. The forest road from Buffalo Creek to Wellington Lake provides a scenic outing for a range of cycling skills and fitness levels.

Head south from your car on Forest Route 543. At about six miles you will merge with Forest Route 550 for four-tenths of a mile. Bear to the left when the road forks (follow signs) and continue another three miles to Wellington Lake. A few hundred yards past the fork look for the Colorado Trail; it is one of the premier mountain bike single tracks in the state.

At Wellington Lake relax and check out The Castle and Windy Peak, then return the way you came, or continue north on 543 for four miles, right (east) on 550 for another four miles to once again join 543. Then, head north back to Buffalo creek.

Forest Route 543 climbs very gradually over the nine miles from Buffalo Creek to Wellington Lake, except the last half mile, which climbs a ridge and gains several hundred vertical feet. There is another short climb out of Wellington Lake heading north on 543, if you choose to complete the Loop.

The Wellington Lake Road can be free of snow in the dead of winter. However, use good judgement before you make the drive; if we have recently experienced a blizzard, then forget it. On a day in March, I began this ride in a t-shirt and finished in snow gear, so go prepared.

DON'T FORGET: Remember, in winter there is no potable water along the route, except snow. In summer, some of the campgrounds have drinking water.

MAPS: U.S.G.S. 7.5 minute: Pine, Green Mountain and Windy Peak. U.S. Forest Service: Pike National Forest.

Tour de Nowhere

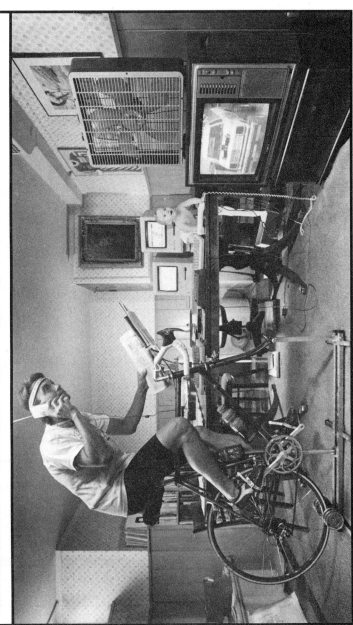

ROCKY MOUNTAIN NEWS

RIDE GUIDE

ROCKY MOUNTAIN NEWS *RIDE GUIDE*

BICYCLE: There are several types of stationary bicycles. Some are made only for pedaling in place, while others, usually referred to as resistance or wind trainers, allow you to mount your road bike on a specially designed stand. It is desirable to do your stationary pedaling on the same bike (and bike seat) that you normally ride on the road. Unfortunately, not all trainers are able to accommodate mountain bikes.

LOCATION: At home, locate your resistance trainer in comfortable surroundings; if you hide it in the coldest, darkest corner of the basement, you'll probably use it less.

However, keep in mind that trainers can make considerable noise (particularly the wind resistance types with fans). And make certain to protect the floor or rug from scuff marks and sweat.

DIFFICULTY: Almost all trainers can be adjusted to provide more or less resistance; shifting gears on your bike also varies the load.

PEDALING IN PLACE: Pedaling a stationary bicycle is an extremely efficient method for maintaining fitness when the winter weather doesn't allow you to ride the roads and trails. Unfortunately, it also can be one of the most tedious, boring tasks of the day – time stands still as if it's quarter to five on Friday afternoon.

Former two-time Coors Classic champion Dale Stetina calls it hateful and now opts for a run in lieu of riding rollers (similar to resistance trainers, but no support for bicycle) to stay fit.

But you don't have to resign yourself to a winter of drudgery. Imagination is the key ingredient in creating distractions that can make resistance training palatable.

If you plan to mount your bike on a trainer during the cold months, a bicycle computer can aid in the quality of your workout, allowing you to monitor speed, distance, cadence, time, etc. (A rear wheel mounting kit might be necessary, depending on type of trainer.)

A computer alone isn't enough to out-sprint the doldrums. A reading stand attached to your handlebars (available through bike shops) adds a whole new dimension to pedaling nowhere. Browse through some of the zillion catalogs you've recently received, finish that spicy novel, or scrutinize a map for a future bike route.

Turn on the stereo (or headphones) and let your favorite music inspire the workout. Unabridged books are available on cassette tape on a rental basis.

Position the telephone within easy reach and make a few calls. Use your Dictaphone to write a letter. Or just keep an eye on the baby. (Baby Dave, in the photo, is not about to crawl off the table – he's only cardboard.)

Tune in a sporting event on the tube or put a movie in the VCR. My overall preferred distraction is viewing bicycle racing footage. Nothing keeps my mind and legs as busy as watching the pros do their thing under race conditions.

Because there's no wind in your face, try a fan to stay cooler and reduce sweat. A headband will minimize the potential mess you'll make of books or the phone.

INDEX OF RIDES
BY DIFFICULTY

Easy

Easy to Moderate

Moderate

Moderate to Difficult

Difficult

INDEX OF RIDES
BY DRIVING TIME
FROM DOWNTOWN DENVER

Under 30 Minutes

Under One Hour

Under One and a Half Hours

Under Two Hours

Over Two Hours